# MASTERING THE

GW00703082

# CRAFT
## BUSINESS

*A business guide for craft artists including starting
a craft venture, marketing, promotion, pricing,
finance, and enjoying the lifestyle.*

## Ann & Bob Phillips

CRAIG
POTTON
PUBLISHING

# AUTHOR ACKNOWLEDGEMENTS

The authors gratefully acknowledge the assistance and advice given so frankly by numerous craft artists in the preparation of this book. Their willingness to share their experiences gave us a better appreciation of the pitfalls that can arise in a craft art venture, and of the ways that craft artists might be helped sidestep them.

ISBN 0 908802 33 1
Published by Craig Potton Publishing, Box 555, Nelson, New Zealand.

First published in 1996
©Text: Ann and Bob Phillips.
©Photographs: credited photographers.

Publishing coordinator: Robbie Burton.
Book Design: One Sky Design.
Editor: David Chowdhury.
Cover Design: Sandipa Gould
Cover photography: ©Julia Brooke-White. Pottery stacked in kiln is that of Richard Parker (large vases) and Ann Verdcourt.

Printed in Hong Kong by Everbest Printing Co. Ltd.

Photography: The publishers wish to thank the craft artists and photographers who kindly allowed their work to be reproduced. All photographs are credited alongside images except for the following used at the beginning of each chapter, and subsequently as detail motifs:
Pg 6, paua and silver bangle by Warwick Freeman (Julia Brooke-White);
Pg 10, turned wooden bowl by Ann and Bob Phillips (Craig Potton);
Pg 14, 'Patches' vase by Richard Parker (Julia Brooke-White);
Pg 20, hammered copper and repoussé silver by Kate Ewing (Julia Brooke-White);
Pg 28, bowl by Melanie Cooper (Julia Brooke-White);
Pg 40, vase by Garry Nash (Julia Brooke-White);
Pg 66, ceramics by Steve Fullmer (Julia Brooke-White);
Pg 74, ceramics by Merilyn Wiseman (Julia Brooke-White);
Pg 80, turned wooden bowl by Ann and Bob Phillips (Ann and Bob Phillips);
Pg 88, 'Winter Quilt' by Marge Hurst (Julia Brooke-White).

# CONTENTS

# FOREWORD

When Ann and Bob Phillips asked me to write a foreword for this (their second) book, I was delighted. As a marketing consultant, I often work with clients in bringing their products to market. Craft artists, like all other entrepreneurs, must continually sharpen their skills in marketing as well as manufacturing in order to achieve business success. In marketing, we are only limited by our imagination.

Bob and Ann provide a good example of what I mean. When I first met them in New York City in 1992, they were on a month-long visit to the United States. They had come as craft trainers and were conducting a full schedule of woodturning workshops in various cities. During their visit, they also checked out museums and speciality shops—always looking for new ideas for marketing their lovely turned wooden bowls, boxes and plates. I was most impressed by their curiosity and creativity.

Only two years later, the Phillips' returned to the US—this time to participate in a variety of art fairs. They arrived in our town (Milwaukee, Wisconsin) in time to visit the annual Lakefront Festival of the Arts, Wisconsin's largest. That evening, we arranged a private showing of their work in our home and invited friends. They announced the upcoming release of their first book. During their stay, the Phillips' tireless itinerary included sales calls at Milwaukee's most prestigious shops. This approach paid off and they got immediate orders. By getting to know their American 'market' first hand, they made many contacts which are providing rewards now, and will for years to come.

Let's take a look at the thinking that prompted their visits here: They were already serving many American customers. Once they identified the bigger American market as an opportunity to increase sales, they needed to figure out how to reach it? They considered who in America would be likely buyers of turned wood products and identified these people as individuals who attend art fairs, shop at specialty stores and buy through upscale mail order catalogues. Next, Ann and Bob asked themselves how they could gain the attention of the people in this market niche.

They decided they could reach them through stores, at art fairs and by becoming recognized authors. As a result of these combined efforts, their contacts have paid off. While their business is located on the other side of the world, they *are* making a name for themselves in our country and elsewhere as authors, craft artists and producers of unique, high quality wood products.

While their somewhat global approach to marketing is working well for them, it may not work for everyone. There are as many twists to marketing as there are products to sell. That's what challenges creative thinking and makes it fun.

When you are working your way though initial plans to market your products, do remember that every craft is different and every company unique. There is no set way. But sound planning helps (and so does a consultation with a marketing expert). It is important to think through the process as an entrepreneur. By so doing, your underlying marketing goals always remain the same: to match the product with potential buyers and provide reasons to buy. Combine this thinking with high standards of product quality, delivery and service and your ability to earn your living as a craft artist is easily within reach.

Karen Frindell Strom,
*President,*
*KFS Creative Services,*
*Milwaukee, Wisconsin, USA*

# INTRODUCTION

*In this book we hope to persuade craft artists to challenge the traditional dogma that they shouldn't pursue professional or commercial success. Our fundamental premise is that taking a professional approach is not incompatible with worthy artistic endeavour. Despite this it's no easy task to convince craft artists to shake what we feel is the limiting and destructive belief that success and worthy endeavour are irreconcilable. Indeed, the very idea of commercial success makes some craft artists shudder — yet when challenged their arguments are confused.*

It seems insidiously easy to accept the conventional outlook that 'true' craft artists must take their place on a higher plane, aloof from the profit motive. That these attitudes are widespread doesn't make them any more tenable. An important point to understand is that as craft artists we have extremely personal, idiosyncratic approaches to our work. There's no reason why our goals and our concepts of success can't be equally individual. Because notions of artistic correctness are extraordinarily influential, many craft artists fail to reach their potential and their talents are wasted or frustrated simply because of half-baked ideas of how a craft artist should behave. This is ludicrous. The straitjacket of 'artistically correct' behaviour has no more to recommend it than did Victorian expectations of ladylike conduct.

Good business sense does *not* stifle creativity. This is a popular misconception that is glib, facile and wrong. Developing organisational skills can in fact be creatively fulfilling and satisfying. An individual who is a competent businessperson as well as a fine craft artist will derive an enormous confidence boost from being in control in both arenas. Some craft artists would even admit that they relish the challenges involved in marketing their work effectively.

## PROFESSIONALISM AND CRAFT ARTISTS

Professionalism means more than just working fulltime, and much more than simply being paid for what you create. It embodies a system of values and ethics, a characteristic dedication, a willingness to take endless pains. Professionalism commands respect whether it be in arts, crafts, medicine or in any other field. Craft artists should always be seeking to portray a professional image embodying confidence and credibility. This is an important point. As craft artists we are intimately and inextricably identified with our work. The impression that we give of ourselves reflects on and in our work—we *are* our work.

Like many craft artists we're deeply suspicious of marketing jargon and principles. The main reason we wrote this book was because we have found that the widely available small business manuals, accounting texts and selling manuals for retailers are rarely appropriate for someone wanting to earn their

Bob and Ann Phillips at work.

living as a craft artist. As practising craft artists we've graduated through an impressive catalogue of learning experiences (some might label them mistakes!)—what we have learned will help you to achieve your ambitions, however diverse those might be.

In this book we shall do our best to persuade you that if we can, you can, so whatever your individual goals may be, it's possible to be sustained by the work you love. It requires effort and commitment, but we hope that the experiences catalogued here will either inspire you to embark on a creative career, or restore confidence in your ability to maintain an artistic livelihood. We begin by helping you sort out what is important to you, how to decide on and work towards personal goals, reconciling creative and professional needs (who you are and what you want). This leads into factors that must be considered when establishing yourself in a craft art venture. The section 'Widening Your Scope' then looks at ways of acquiring and developing skills to add to your repertoire, including photography for the reasonably impecunious craft artists with only basic camera equipment. We guide you through the minefield of administrative matters—such thorny questions as 'how can I price my work?', 'how can I talk to a bank about a loan?'.

In the chapter on marketing, our basic rationale is that you don't have to stay poor in order to retain your artistic integrity. We look at practical examples of a variety of selling methods, and provide guidance on choosing an appropriate balance of marketing approaches for your situation.

Recognising that we all have to come to terms with the outside world, we provide a light but informative treatment of topics concerning the craft artist: advocacy, promotion, public speaking, education, dissemination of shared values. In a troubleshooting chapter we offer anecdotes illustrating common problems—even if it's not always possible to learn from others' mistakes it's very human to enjoy reading about them—and discuss ways of dealing with difficulties as they arise.

While working at it is vital, the most important aspect for us is enjoying the craft artist's lifestyle. We discuss what makes the lifestyle special, and give tips on maintaining balance and enthusiasm.

In conclusion this book will show you that it's not incredibly difficult to earn your living as a craft artist. We promise that the feeling of fulfilment and achievement more than repays the relatively minor effort involved in coping with necessary evils such as paperwork!

Shavings fly at Bob's lathe

*Craig Potton*

# TAKING STOCK

*If you're considering a career as a craft artist, or if you're an established craft artist hoping to improve your standard of living, a good first step is to take stock of your reasons for pursuing a creative profession. Jot these reasons down. You need not reveal your reasoning to anyone else, so be honest in pinning down what appeals to you about being a professional craft artist. This exercise is carried out just for you, to clarify your ambitions and desires.*

When you've finished you might feel that what's important to you won't be considered important by others. Don't be put off—remember these are your priorities and goals and they are no less valid for being offbeat! Ultimately, you answer only to yourself. Your current priorities may seem weird to an outsider, and in a year or so they may even seem weird to you. This exercise is neither binding nor permanent, but is as mobile and flexible as you and your evolving ideas.

Conversely you might be tempted to view your listed priorities as pretty mundane or too conventional perhaps for an artist with a capital 'A'. Again, don't be swayed by expectations. Try not to override your true opinions by fitting them to some idealised notion of what your aspirations should be!

To help you, we asked a range of craft artists to explain what motivated them to pursue a creative venture. Their responses are listed below:

- to make money
- to become famous/immortal through my work
- to create meaningful work for myself
- to gain more satisfaction from my life
- to change my life in response to a major upheaval
- to enjoy my life more than at present
- to create items of timeless beauty
- to escape from a tedious or unhappy work environment
- to spend more time on what I enjoy and do well
- to have a greater sense of achievement in life
- to use my art to become financially independent

Some of these aims are challenging, others may seem mundane. Don't be in a hurry to make value judgements. The responses to our questions reflected different circumstances, pressures and abilities—some were craft artists with a pressing need to support themselves and a family, some were emerging from art college for a first taste of their own studio, others were simply trying to make sense of their lives by finding new directions.

Your own thoughts could parallel some of the above or be totally unrelated. Note down aspirations that apply to you. What drives you, what motivates you? Try to understand your 'vision'. Give honest answers—remember no-one but you need see this assessment, so you have no pressure to impress anyone with what might seem to be suitably worthy ambitions for a true artist.

Next, try to evaluate honestly, and for your own circumstances, just how realistic some of your ambitions are likely to be in practice. Be optimistic, but temper this optimism with self-knowledge—no-one can carry out this exercise better than you.

We thought it interesting that several craft artists mentioned a major jolt or upset in their personal life as a motivating factor. Some for example had reached what felt like a watershed in their life. The sense of urgency to achieve something creatively worthwhile before they died was their particular spur. Others had become frustrated by their regular employment to the extent they felt themselves to be marking time until they could get down to paint... or sculpt... or whatever.

The personal stocktake is a simple exercise which you can usefully carry out again from time to time in order to keep yourself on track. You'll often find yourself straying from your initial aims. This doesn't necessarily matter, because goals become modified too. Things are not static. What is important though is to ensure that the way things are going is still what you want to happen. Are you generally happy? If not, then what steps can you take to get back in tune with your original aspirations?

## REALISING
## YOUR HOPES

Having asked what motivated craft artists, we then asked how their initial hopes and ambitions measured up in practice. Some conceded that the reality was different from that which they'd visualised. Those who expected to escape a dull job now said that they appreciated how much routine exists in any job—self-employed creative artist or not! Those who anticipated being in charge said they now saw the truth in the adage that the 'self' employed in fact work for their customers! Independence is often a matter of degree! A frequent admission was the failure to foresee the tremendous personal commitment and extra work that self-employment—in the early stages at least—would mean to them and their families.

Not that the effort involved is an arduous slog—let's be clear that this is far

Photo: Julia Brooke-White

from the case. If it were true, then all of us would certainly be doing something else! Earning a living as a craft artist offers the chance to be both creative and financially independent through doing something that we enjoy—what could be more ideal?

The point we make is that anyone who believes their lives will fall magically into place as soon as they call themselves a craft artist is doomed to disillusionment. There are aspects of being a professional craft artist which fall into the 'necessary evils' category and we shall deal with them in this book under the conviction that it is better to cope with them rather than ignore them until they overtake us and cause our downfall!

Realism doesn't mean pessimism. Keep in mind that highs and lows, peaks and troughs are completely normal in even the largest enterprise. The odd lousy week happens, so don't over-react and think you're inept and a failure, or doing it all wrong when such times come about. Learn from them where you can; if they're not anything you can alter, put them behind you and move on! Talking to craft artists it is clear that as a group, we can be pretty hard on ourselves, so try to be reasonable. It is not reasonable, for example, to make yourself miserable because you didn't immediately set the world on fire with your latest designs. Success means achieving what you want to happen. It can be as simple as being personally fulfilled in your work. We discuss 'success' in more depth in the following chapter.

# BEFORE YOU START YOUR BUSINESS

*SHOULD YOU WORK FROM HOME OR A studio? What about craft collectives? Have you defined what success means to you? These are questions that you should consider seriously before you plunge into your craft art venture.*

# WORKING FROM HOME OR FROM A STUDIO?

Having sorted out the 'whys' in your personal stocktake, often the next choice to be made when planning your enterprise is 'where'. Working from home has many advantages and most craft art ventures are home-based. In fact practically all craft artists begin their ventures at home. The attractions include lower establishment costs: no commuting costs, and no extra rent or rates to meet.

Working from home offers the added convenience of being in your own environment with both the comforts and distractions that presents! Provided your local regulations permit, a home-based venture has much to recommend it. Before mentally transforming your home, check the local authority zoning requirements. The law quite rightly protects occupiers of residential neighbourhoods from activities which could disturb them or be otherwise detrimental to a residential area. If you are a sculptor with a taste for the gigantic, some of your work processes may have a substantial impact on your neighbour! It pays to plan ahead. We know of several examples where a creative venture, like Topsy, 'just growed', and suddenly those concerned found themselves saddled with unwelcome problems.

Be optimistic though. People can be very reasonable and even if your activity is of a sort that will affect others, and is not a permitted use in your area, you may be granted clearance to carry on, perhaps with conditions such as hours of work attached. The onus will be on you to persuade others that your activities won't have a detrimental impact. Nowadays perhaps the security aspect of having someone present all day in a commuter suburb where houses are empty during office hours would be a persuasive appeal to neighbours!

Encouragingly for craft artists, town planning regulations in many parts of the world have become much more flexible and accommodating of home-based ventures in recognition of worldwide trends in working patterns. If you think about it from a historical perspective, it is only relatively recently (since the industrial revolution) that the pattern of leaving home to go to work became the norm.

Working from home has great advantages, but let us look too, at some of the problems which occasionally arise.

## Isolation

The need for regular human contact is a deep-seated one and if you'll be working alone you should consider the effects of isolation on your work. We have colleagues and friends who have left for other work for no other reason but loneliness. One had stuck it out for nine years, and only returned to his venture after an 18 month break. Until we experienced this in our own circle we had never given any thought to isolation. Since becoming aware of it, we have heard of similar instances where working in isolation has proved too high a cost.

## Dealing with isolation

If you know yourself to be a social animal, a good option is to join a cooperative (see below). Form one yourself if there is none available and you see a potential in your area. Find out if a support network for homeworkers or 'teleworkers' is operating in your area. Such networks are springing up in response to the needs of home office workers, but they may also be a helpful source of contact for the lone craft artist. Partnerships work well in most craft ventures—clearly it's worked in our own case because we had never considered the problem of isolation!

When establishing your venture, don't therefore, confine your plans to workshop/studio matters. Give due thought to your need for social contact. You need work space, but your personal space is equally important.

# CO-OPS AND COLLECTIVES— SHARING FACILITIES WITH OTHER CRAFT ARTISTS

Becoming involved with co-ops or collectives is an option generally taken up by the semi-serious or fulltime craft artist (although we have friends involved in collectives and cooperatives who are neither) and suits those who enjoy the social aspects of a shared enterprise with others. More time can be devoted to your work without distractions and interruptions. A craft cooperative or collective is a jointly owned and run craft enterprise. Craft artists working cooperatively with others sharing similar aspirations and motivations can more easily achieve goals which they would struggle to meet working alone. The different skills and strengths of the members can often produce a highly successful joint enterprise. From our own involvement in cooperatives we rate the essential ingredient for success as good communication between members. Nowhere is this more evident than in decision making.

If you are new to the process of group decision making, be prepared to call on your reserves of tolerance. Decision making by consensus sounds wonderful, but in practice can be both more protracted and frustrating than you would believe possible.

In most cooperatives, the stated ideal is that all responsibilities are shared democratically. In our experience the tasks can be arranged so that members take care of areas best suited to their skills. A good example is in bookkeeping where one member may look after the paperwork for the whole group. This will work so long as a balance is maintained so every member feels fairly done by.

In every stable cooperative we know of there has been a formal agreement of some form drawn up and adhered to. Such an agreement might cover basic rules, shares and commitments, together with agreed arrangements for resigning members, and procedures for admitting new members.

## SUCCESS AND THE CRAFT ARTIST

Before you establish, it's important to sort out just what 'success' means to you. As one stereotype of success would have it, successful people are obsessive, selfish tyrants who sacrifice ethics and relationships to achieve their overweening ambitions! Allowing for some slight overstatement, is there some vestige of truth in this to you? Do you have some sneaking belief that success is not a worthy aim, that successful people are fundamentally ruthless and hard-nosed; they'd have to be wouldn't they? deep down anyway? to be successful, powerful? Does this strike a chord? If so, then deal with this spectre first. Success is what you determine it shall be. Try to clarify just what that is to your own personal satisfaction.

Harking back to your personal stocktake, accept that there will be widely diverging opinions of what constitutes success. Deal with this simple idea and

Working partnerships are a good counter against isolation difficulties. Bruce Hamlin and Rosie Little of Estuary Arts.

*Craig Potton*

you can face a lot of the double standards relating to craft artist ventures with equanimity.

For some of us, success will be the conventionally accepted version—public recognition, and/or making a lot of money (the two don't always come as a package deal!). For others it will be the creation of beautiful objects in order to satisfy personal ambition, achieving a secure and stable income, or creating a pleasant and varied working life.

Generally success will be a combination of these and other outcomes— essentially whatever we most want to happen. Being successful is achieving what you've set out to do. Setting both short and long term targets ensures that you reward yourself with achievement as you progress. In our work we like to set specific targets for the short term—successfully meeting these targets is almost like a game, but more of this in a later chapter.

An example of a specific target for success could be to mount a solo exhibition of your work. Such short term targets will give you a deserved feeling of achievement and lead you progressively to more general long term goals such as national recognition. Make your short term targets fairly realistic and use long term targets to stretch your ideas more!

If your private goal is to make money, don't feel it's an indefensible ambition. Money is not intrinsically unworthy, its acquisition need not be in opposition to creative and artistic goals. You don't have to starve in a garret to be true to your art unless that lifestyle has particular appeal for you. (Although privately we suspect that living hand to mouth is unlikely to promote creative inspiration because you'd be too busy worrying about the very basics necessary for existence.)

We hope this has persuaded those of you uncomfortable with fame and fortune that you don't need a Jekyll and Hyde personality to be successful. Success won't change you into a monster. In fact, on the way to achieving your ambitions, you'll possibly be changed for the better! Your personal qualities are liable to be developed and strengthened, for you'll need new skills and attributes, specifically, perseverance (sticking at it) and self-confidence (faith in yourself and your abilities). These won't appear overnight, but if for example you haven't handled a particularly testing situation very well on your first attempt, put it behind you (while resolving to make a better job of it next time). Be tolerant of yourself. We can't all be fantastically brilliant, stunningly incisive and frighteningly efficient, at least not all the time!

## THE CRAFT LIFESTYLE
## —A LONG WAY FROM UTOPIA

Remarks from customers visiting our gallery like "aren't you lucky to be doing what you enjoy", "must be wonderful to escape the rat race", "I dream of getting away from it all like this", lead us to suspect that people hold a fantasy view of life as a craft artist. Whilst we've never delved into these wistful imaginings it's clear to us that they view our existence as a Utopian idyll!

If you haven't yet sampled self-employment as a craft artist then bear in mind that it won't be roses all the way. There will always be hassles and pressures, but nothing that you won't be able to handle.

# ADMINISTRATION AND YOUR ART – PAPERWORK

*IF THE PERSONAL COST OF WORKING ALONE IS often overlooked by craft artists, even less attention is likely to be focused on setting up the administrative side of your venture, in other words, dealing with the paperwork. Aspiring craft artists who visit our studio and gallery never express equal interest in viewing the office!*

From comparing notes with our colleagues, it seems this is typical—a telling attitude, and one with which we are in complete sympathy. However, you should accept now that some paperwork will be a necessary part of your work, and anyway, if you don't know what's happening in your venture, who does? You should aim to do what is necessary, but no more. By having simple procedures, streamlined so that you do the minimum that you need to, you'll zip through the paperwork rather than flounder in it!

Often craft artists declare they can't handle paperwork. In our experience this is untrue. It's really not a matter of being unable to do the paperwork, more a case that they find paperwork monumentally unappealing! Once the individual can be convinced that the tedious tasks can be quickly and painlessly dealt with, previously insurmountable problems evaporate. Our philosophy is that if (like us) you detest paperwork the best way around it is to deal with it so efficiently that it is completed before you know it .

The following guidelines will enable you to establish an easily-handled basic support system for your creative venture without needing to resort to unintelligible treatises on business accounting. The thought that we cling to is that most paperwork is easy in the sense that it's not a task that requires intense or original thought.

We start with our three tips for coping with day-to-day paperwork on your own, and then move on to look at how you can use outside assistance as and when the need arises.

## THREE SURVIVAL RULES FOR RELUCTANT BOOK KEEPERS

1. Keep everything relevant to your business, and this must include all invoices, receipts and statements. Conversely, throw away at once everything that is irrelevant before it obscures what you need to keep! Being ruthless at an early stage (usually when the mail arrives) saves an enormous amount of effort.

2. Maintain a filing system that enables easy retrieval of invoices, receipts, statements and other papers that you keep. (We'll give you some tips on filing later in the section.)

| DATE | DETAIL | CH No | BANK AMOUNT | MATERIALS | CAR | ADMIN. | FREIGHT | REPAIRS | SELLING COSTS | OTHER | AMOUNT | DATE | DETAIL (CUSTOMER) | INV. | BANKED |
|---|---|---|---|---|---|---|---|---|---|---|---|---|---|---|---|
| 6 1 | ABC SUPPLIES | 01 | 700 00 | 700 00 | | | | | | | | 11 1 | FGH GIFTS | 33 | 750 00 |
| 12 1 | PHONE COMPANY | 02 | 50 50 | | | | | | | PHONE | 50 50 | 15 1 | GALLERY 21 | 34 | 400 00 |
| 15 1 | XY GARAGE | 03 | 100 00 | | 100 00 | | | | | | | 22 1 | M. SMITH | 35 | 550 00 |
| 20 1 | PERSONAL CASH | 04 | 200 00 | | | | | | | DRAWING | 200 00 | 23 1 | GALLERY Z | 36 | 150 00 |
| 25 1 | FIXIT CO. | 05 | 106 20 | | | | | 106 20 | | | | | …AND SO ON | | |
| 29 1 | EXPO LTD | 06 | 140 00 | | | | | | 140 00 | | | | | | |
| | PLUS OTHER ENTRIES | | | | | | | | | | | | | | |
| | AS APPLICABLE | | | | | | | | | | | | | | |
| TOTALS | TOTAL EXPENSE FOR JANUARY | | 1296 70 | 700 00 | 100 00 | | | 106 20 | 140 00 | | 250 50 | | TOTAL EARNINGS FOR JANUARY | | 1850 00 |

ALL THESE TOTALS SHOULD EQUATE TO THE GRAND TOTAL (THEY ARE A DETAILED BREAKDOWN OF EXPENSES)

**AN EXAMPLE OF A SIMPLE CASHBOOK LAYOUT**

3. Start using a simple cashbook, with headings made out for your incomings and outgoings. Then make sure you fill in the spaces! (We will show you a typical model, but the system you use is important only so far as it must be simple enough to use easily, without having to backtrack all the time to figure out where everything should go! Having a headed-up space waiting for entries means that you're halfway through the job before you start and don't have to exercise any decision-making about where entries should be made.)

In addition to these rules, always be on the lookout for ways to save time. Aim to cut out all but that which is absolutely essential to the smooth running of your enterprise.

Some examples: 1. Open a completely separate cheque account for all business expenses and payments. This keeps financial recordkeeping very simple and means there's no muddle between personal and business finances.

2. If you're someone who forgets to keep records of your correspondence

(embarrassing when a query is made later), use a duplicate book (the type that makes carbon copies) to record all communications with clients and suppliers. This immediately eliminates a filing stage and is easy to refer to when there's a query raised.

3. If you use a facsimile machine, don't waste time typing if you find it a chore. No-one will think worse of you for (clear) handwritten communication. Indeed, we find such notes often receive more immediate attention than typed letters.

Poor recordkeeping is at the heart of many problems that crop up so it's good practice to jot down things that confuse you. If you are unsure of something, note it down and ask about it as soon as you can. Get minor worries sorted out before they grow and you become bogged down in the problem. Often a fellow craft artist will have the answer. At least when muddles arise, if you've noted down the cause, your helper will have something to work on.

However little you feel like facing up to paperwork, just do it. 'Shoebox' record-keeping is better than nothing, but the time taken to sort it all out will again cost you more in money and hassle than learning to cope with a system of sorts as we have outlined.

## FILING ...
## OR 'WHAT TO KEEP WHERE
## SO THAT YOU CAN FIND IT AGAIN'

We've talked about the necessity of storing records such as invoices, statements and so on. The following suggestions on filing may save you from a descent into chaos! The only essential is that you create a system you're able to use which allows you to find documents without a house-search worthy of the gestapo!

1. Devise a way of filing that suits you. If you like lots of folders containing fairly narrowly defined topics that's fine. If you're more of a 'lumper' than a 'splitter' you'll probably find it easier to have just a few folders. Ringbinders are good for statements, invoices, receipts and correspondence as they bind every-thing securely, and you can flick through rapidly when you need to trace something.

2. File anywhere but on the same bench, table or other flat surface you use for your paperwork. If you have to clear a space to start work, the odds are that you won't do either paperwork or filing!

3. Finally, we've said it before and we'll say it again. Don't keep what you don't need. Get ruthless. A major spring-clean showed us that a good percentage of filed material was outdated and unnecessary. Our shelves were cluttered and every search for material was made that much longer because we had to wade through masses of irrelevant material to find what we wanted. You'll keep paper recyclers well supplied, especially with all the unsolicited mail you're likely to receive from companies hell-bent on deforesting the world by catalogue production!

If, despite these dire warnings, you simply cannot bring yourself to discard written material of dubious worth, then at least store your 'just in case' treasures where they won't impede you. 'Miscellaneous' is a very useful category. These few tips really will enable you to have a smooth-running paperwork support for your venture without making hard work of it. The aim is to clear the way for you to concentrate on the far more enjoyable aspects of your creative life.

# USING ADVISORS

So far we have looked at how you can maintain a good overview of your venture. Doing basic paperwork for yourself enables you to remain fairly independent and know how things are going without needing to consult experts to find out if the news is good or bad! Occasionally, however, you will have to call on the detailed knowledge of experts such as accountants, if only once a year. This doesn't mean handing over all responsibility and control to someone else—tempting as this might sound, total surrender in this way is a *bad* idea.

### Using advisors—how and when

Too high a dependence on others is unwise (as well as astronomically expensive if they are paid advisors!). On the other hand none of us have infinite knowledge and we all need good advice on occasions. The trick is to decide what kind of help and how much you need at a particular time. Whilst your venture is your own, knowing when to call on expert assistance, and then using that advice, is important.

### Advice for free

Depending on your need for information, agencies such as consumer groups or citizens advice bureaux may be a useful first line of general enquiry. It will also be worth finding out if there's a small business advisory centre near you, or if there are advisors employed by the tax department to assist you with tax matters (you may feel a tax advisor is the last person you ought to approach, but look at it this way: the more successful you become, the more the tax department gets. Thus it's in their best interests that you do well!). These opportunities, where they exist, should be used fully. While they may not eliminate your need for paid specialist advice, what you learn from these subsidised sources will enable you to be better prepared yourself. Armed with extra knowledge you'll spend less time, and so less money, with your paid advisor.

### ...and paid advice

We may resent the cost of expert advisors, but good advice is worth the expense in avoided mistakes and wasted time saved. That being so, try not to begrudge the costs! Ensure your advisor is a good one. They come in grades of good, bad, and indifferent, just like the rest of us!

### Safeguards

Without being too cynical:
1. Never trust blindly, however personable the expert is.
2. Ensure that you keep copies of all work done for you.
3. Always maintain personal control of your bank account.

Ceramics by Christine Boswijk
*Julia Brooke-White*

Expert assistance may consist of having your bookwork done for you. Equally though, it may involve teaching you how to set up and operate an administrative routine appropriate to your enterprise. For example, under the guidance of a sympathetic accountant willing to help you set up easily handled systems, your accountancy fees should gradually reduce as you take on more of the responsibility for bookkeeping yourself.

## CHOOSING
## AN ADVISOR

When it comes to choosing your advisor—and the main one will probably be an accountant—then it pays to shop around. Ask other craft artists for their recommendations. This way you can narrow your search to those experienced with, and sympathetic to enterprises similar to yours.

Having chosen your advisor, it is equally vital to ensure that you understand what you expect of one another. Many craft artists we spoke to felt they had been ripped off by accountants. However, on further investigation, most of the rip-off cases stemmed from misunderstandings on both sides where neither craft artist nor accountant had been sufficiently clear on what was expected of each other.

Overcharging is often a case of a 'Rolls Royce' accounts job being carried out for a 'Trabant' enterprise. A couple of cautionary tales are outlined below as examples of this situation.

The first involved a craft artist who simply needed a clear statement of figures once a year for her tax return. Instead of this, she was provided with a sophisticated state-of-the-art financial analysis that was out of all proportion to the scale of her activity.

After a period of recrimination she paid the bill and instantly moved downmarket to a 'bush accountant' who she finds does a good job for a fraction of the fee.

In the second and similar case the craft artist was a designer of clothes for children. Being the mother of a young family she particularly wanted to earn from home, and began a very small part-time enterprise. Her bookwork was prepared for her at a time when she was barely out of the hobby stage and the fee came as a horrible shock! (At least, she says, she never resents paying her new consultant's bills, as several years down the track his fees are less than the first fee, so seem remarkably modest.)

Arguably, professional advisors could use more common sense in their approach, but these two examples should alert you to the need to make your position crystal clear. Here are some tips to help just in case:

1. Find out what fees other craft artists pay. Checking with friends operating on a similar scale should reduce the risk of receiving a nightmarish fee.

2. Discuss the scope of your venture at an initial interview with your advisor before any work is done on your behalf. An estimate of likely cost can be discussed—a blanket refusal should make you nervous. Be assertive enough to ask for an estimate of fees before you make a commitment. An accountant who handles ventures similar to yours should be able to provide an estimate.

3. State your requirements clearly (from notes if that helps you). For example if you want to learn to do most of the paperwork yourself, be quite blunt about it. Then if this ambition isn't well received you can move elsewhere!

4. Try, as far as possible, to give a definite guide as to the amount of work you want done. Do you want a wide range of business advice, help with securing finance, preparation of business plans and so on? Do you want only basic tax-return preparation? Be very clear at the outset, lest you receive the full gamut of services, with a bill to match!

## CHOOSING
## THE RIGHT ADVISOR

Whilst the craft artist/advisor relationship is a professional one, most of us prefer to work with someone we like and are at ease with. If you aren't on the same wavelength as your advisor, if the advice given is never explained in terms that you can understand, and if you find yourself doing a lot of pointless paperwork, then it's time to make a move. Finding someone you can work comfortably with will make the whole affair easier for you, and in the long run you'll cover your advisor's fees in the money that you have saved. Also, your investment in advice will have given you the confidence to better cope with the administrative side of your craft venture.

# ADDING NEW SKILLS TO YOUR REPERTOIRE

*THERE'S A RATHER GLIB MAXIM WHICH goes something like "you cannot be taught, you can only ever be helped to learn" and while this is rather clichéd, it's also difficult to argue with. We all need to learn in order to grow and develop – and this process doesn't start and end with your initial formal training.*

By taking advantage of every opportunity you reasonably can to enhance your personal abilities you'll avoid becoming stale and devoid of inspiration. Being open to new ideas will keep you flexible and adaptable, and therefore a better candidate for personal growth and development, and for success in your own creative enterprise.

What makes this path difficult is that, in whatever area we wish to improve it's first necessary to acknowledge what weaknesses you need to work on and to make a time commitment to make that improvement possible.

Try to paint with a broad brush—take time to interest yourself in opportunities for inspiration from varied sources. It doesn't necessarily matter if there's no direct relevance to your work. We have found that a good presenter with enthusiasm for a topic can not only entertain, but also inspire new lines of thought. You won't score every time of course, but you've lost nothing.

A particular example from our situation is the time we wandered into an art history lecture while travelling overseas. Art history has no direct relevance to our medium so the topic (some of the great master painters) wasn't riveting, but the speaker was, and because of that we stayed to listen. His view was that many of the 'great artists', far from being 'above' cross commercialism, painted very specifically for a market. Some of his examples were rather shocking, for in his version some of the classic paintings we studied at school actually verged on child pornography when considered in context. It was a salacious but fascinating viewpoint, and so plausible! The artists were prolific and their buyers could well have been the dirty raincoat brigade—albeit well-heeled!

This knowledgeable, witty and intriguing lecturer set us thinking about marketing. In art/craft it's not easy to incorporate commercial needs with the perceived image of a craft artist. Here was circumstantial evidence at least, to suggest that some of those regarded as models of artistic genius, actually target-marketed very effectively!

Whilst learning specific new skills or techniques is relatively straightforward, developing your 'eye' or perceptive faculties and a 'feeling' for good design are rather more complex processes. A good starting point is to expand your learning experiences. This often gives you a renewed vision and a different slant on your own work endeavours.

# WORKSHOPS, SEMINARS AND SHORT COURSES

Attending workshops and courses can be extremely worthwhile, though putting aside time for them can be hard. Special interest workshops or pressure-cooker short courses are a good option for those with time limitations. A good tip is to arrange an expert to give a lecture to a group you belong to. The quality of the speaker is all important—we've attended sessions on planning where we agreed afterwards the drawcard couldn't have organised the proverbial brewery outing!

Colleges of education, polytechnics and other similar institutes may be persuaded to run short block courses on design, photography, whatever, if there are enough people with a common interest in the topic requesting it. This can

Hoglund's Glassblowing Studio

*Craig Potton*

be an excellent way of making best use of visiting artists-in-residence.

Seminars are normally fun to attend and refreshing. There are pros and cons when evaluating them as a learning environment. Firstly the numbers attending can be very large—this is good for interaction, questioning and brainstorming, but not so valuable if you want to study closely one person's approach or philosophy. You may find much of the benefit you gain is derived from your fellow participants.

Remember too that taking yourself away and putting yourself in a different situation is a good way to give yourself a complete break from your own environment if you feel you're getting in a rut. The more sociable, and generally more active learning occurs when learning involves others. This can range from individual or group tuition up to conferences or seminars. A good seminar or conference should leave you dizzy with new ideas and inspiration!

## INDIVIDUAL TUITION

Individual tuition can involve rapid and intensive learning of particular new skills. An example could be where a highly skilled production craftsperson has been lured out of retirement to help you acquire some of his or her techniques.

If you wish to become a quick and accurate production weaver for example, close attention to the working style of a virtuoso can be invaluable, particularly for learning little tricks of the trade which never made the books!

## JOINING A GROUP

Joining associations of people with a common interest provides a further opportunity for learning. These might include art societies, writing circles, cultural tourism associations—wherever your own interests overlap. Guest speakers at these associations can introduce you to new ideas, new ways of looking at old ideas, or just make you think! Take an active part, but be reasonable. Don't bone up the night before in order to discomfort the speaker with esoteric queries to flaunt your own erudition. It could be you in the hot seat one day!

## TELLING YOUR STORY

On the other side of the coin, speaking to interested groups yourself is a skill worth developing. What better way to make arts accessible than have the public meet and hear the artist? The important trick is to pitch your talk to the appropriate level to get your message across. Err on the simplistic side because it's easy to lose an audience. (see section on public speaking in Chapter 5, page 63)

## OTHER LEARNING AVENUES

Always remain open to new learning avenues, even if they seem far from your immediate work. You will find that new knowledge can often be more relevant than you supposed. We can illustrate this from our experience of an evening class in calligraphy we undertook for fun one gloomy winter. The course, although just a short introduction to what is an art form in itself, was well taught, and thanks to the tutor's infectious enthusiasm we discovered the pleasure of the calm, rhythmic fluency of the calligraphic artist! We discussed this after the course with a potter who explained that practising different 'hands' gave her a fluency which she was able to incorporate when applying decoration to her pots. In some of the art deco style involving brushwork decoration, she found this new fluency improved her styles considerably! And in the same way we found our decorative work benefitted from our exposure to calligraphic discipline.

Carving by Filipe Tohi
*Julia Brooke-White*

This overview type of exposure to a new field won't make you instantly proficient, but if it's well presented, should provide you with new perspectives. Nothing that you learn is entirely irrelevant, however off-track the new knowledge seems at the time!

Another example: a glassworkers' group invited us to a talk given by an interior designer who specialised in lighting effects. The talk was naturally slanted to displaying glassware, but listening to the viewpoint of a design consultant gave us pointers too. Using different light intensities to create different areas of emphases, oblique lighting to emphasise particular features of texture or form, for example, were universally applicable. We always now look at the lighting methods in staged exhibitions to see how successfully lighting has been used! So, while many of the new things you learn won't be immediately useful—they will surface when need dredges them up!

## COLLABORATIONS WITH OTHER CRAFT ARTISTS

Collaborations with craft artists in other media can provide a lot of fun as well as expand your horizons. Perhaps you'll have the aptitude to incorporate the different medium into your work, or you may prefer direct collaboration with another artist/craftsperson in creating a body of work reflecting your shared talents. If you don't win over the critics, at least you'll have a sympathetic shoulder when the reviews come in!

# PHOTOGRAPHING YOUR WORK

Learning the basics of photography is a good skill to add to your repertoire because at some stage you'll need good photos of your work. Like it or not, there will be occasions when your work stands or falls on the quality of these images. If, for example, you are asked to submit photos for a juried show or exhibition, a few dog-eared photos showing examples of work shot on the kitchen table will simply lose you the jury fee (many organisations ask for a non-refundable deposit to pay for their selection or administration costs).

To indicate the importance of good photography, remember that exhibits for some exhibitions are chosen by a panel of jurors viewing slides of craft artists' work. Typically, jurors are drawn from artists working in a variety of media, together with curators of art museums and galleries. During their (often brief) selection sessions, slides from each exhibitor may be projected simultaneously. For example, if five slides are requested from each applicant there will be five projectors set up. Clearly, since the panel views large numbers of slides, no single slide is likely to be on screen for long, so your image must have impact!

More and more exhibitors use professionally photographed transparencies (slides) to enhance their chances of acceptance. We spent an interesting day with an art photographer who specialises in this field. At his studio cartons of work arrive from all over the country, sent by craftspeople needing eyecatching shots of their pieces. He provided a complete service, right down to custom-made labels for slides. The fact that he has been able to specialise in this way speaks volumes for the value craft artists place on having high quality pictures at their disposal.

Not all of us, however, have the funds or the deadline margins that allow us to use specialist photographers. We believe that everyone should at least *try* to photo-graph their own work. As with other skills, you are bound to improve with practice, and you could well become a reasonably competent photographer in the process.

Our own early attempts with photography were truly awful but, as with other skills, the more practice we put in the better we became. A good first step would be to join a local camera club where you will glean useful advice, and you'll perhaps find a sympathetic and interested member prepared to help you out.

For those of you who feel unable to learn or are simply uninterested in the language of apertures, exposures and 'f' stops, we have put together a set of simple guidelines for absolute beginners.

Basic equipment you'll need:

- A camera and tripod;
- Neutral coloured card or fabric for backdrop material;
- A light source for indoor photography, either a flash or a cheap halogen lamp. The latter must be used in conjunction with a blue filter (blue cellophane is an inexpensive option here) to prevent the image becoming over warm, ie too yellow;
- Props such as reflective materials and supports for your pieces that can be assembled as and when required.

We assume you own a standard 'point and shoot' 35mm camera with simple focus adjustments or auto-focusing. Investing in a tripod is worth the small cost—you'll probably find a second-hand trade-in at your local camera shop. With this basic equipment you'll take adequate photographs of your work—heresy though this may seem to the purists!

Professional props and backdrop materials are expensive, but with a bit of creative adaptation you can improvise with little or no-cost materials such as tin foil, old fabrics, umbrellas and so on.

A word on film. Your choice of film will determine the quality of the image, and some experimentation will be required with different film types. Each film has an ASA or ISO rating—those with low (50-100 ASA/ISO) ratings produce truer colours, and those with high ratings (200 ASA/ISO upwards) tend to produce grainier-looking images. Also worth experimenting with is the variation in colour between different brands of film; some films tend to enhance colours to give a brighter effect.

### Where to start

Having sourced your camera and tripod you are ready for your first session. The first choice you will face is whether to shoot indoors or outside. We suggest that you start by working in an outdoor setting. Providing the weather obliges, there will be few lighting worries to complicate your early attempts. Ideal conditions to try out your photography are bright yet overcast days. Essentially, such conditions provide the very scattered light which reduces shadows, giving the effect of many light sources, rather than one. In these conditions all you have to do is line up the shot!

## Backgrounds

Organise a simple background that won't distract the eye away from the subject of your photograph. A neutral-coloured card or uncreased fabric (pinned behind so that no edges show in the frame of your photograph) is a safe option. Excellent for this purpose are old roller blinds which are robust, non-creasing, and easily stored.

## Keep Records

The number one tip for your first excursion into photography is to take notes of what you did to set up each shot. Now this may sound boring, but in the long run it will be the single most helpful factor in improving the overall quality of your photography. Keeping records will identify the ploys that worked well and those that failed. When you find a setup that works you will then achieve consistently good results by repeating what you'd done earlier, and avoid wasting film repeating forgotten blunders!

As you improve you may want to develop more sophisticated shots rather than those that merely record your work accurately. Try experimenting with your work set against textured backgrounds—neutral grey gravels or driftwood are other outdoor backdrop options you might like to pursue.

## The indoor photo studio

The down side of outdoor photography is that you can't control the conditions. Hope for suitable lighting on the day you elect to take photographs, and very likely the sun will shine bright in a cloudless sky, casting strong shadows. You can get around some conditions, for example by using reflective materials to direct light into shadowed areas, or by introducing extra lighting. In bad weather though, you may have to cope with changing conditions and if they deteriorate you'll be forced indoors in any case. On bad weather days, or if there are no suitable outdoor areas available, indoor photography is the next step. Here the aim is to replicate good outdoor conditions indoors.

Working indoors you face the basic problem of providing good lighting for your shots. A simple option is to make the light source as diffuse as possible—a

## SIMPLE DIFFUSERS FOR PHOTOGRAPHY AT HOME

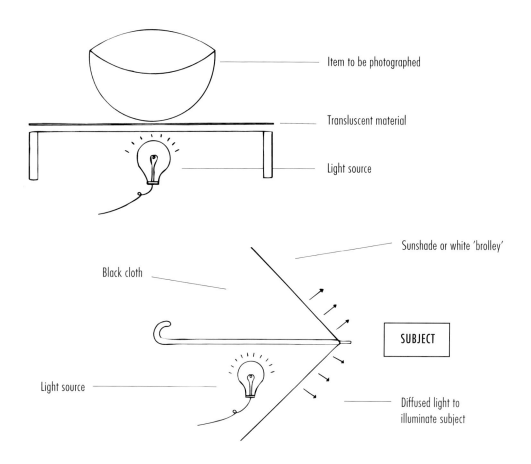

Item to be photographed

Transluscent material

Light source

Sunshade or white 'brolley'

Black cloth

Light source

SUBJECT

Diffused light to illuminate subject

professional photographer would use reflectors and commercially made diffusers amongst a host of other expensive props, but you can improvise with cheaper alternatives. A cheap white sunshade/umbrella can be used as a diffuser for example, and this can be made even more effective by sewing a hood of black fabric around the spokes. A lamp can be clamped within this as shown in the sketch.

A diffuser to soften shadows can also be created by using suitably supported translucent materials. Old polycarbonate cladding, net curtain and drafting paper are just a few ideas. Any material which allows some light to filter through can be tried, so have a look around and see what you have to hand. Keep your notes and you will soon have an idea of a workable system which meets your particular needs.

A light table makes a useful prop when you want to photograph your work lit

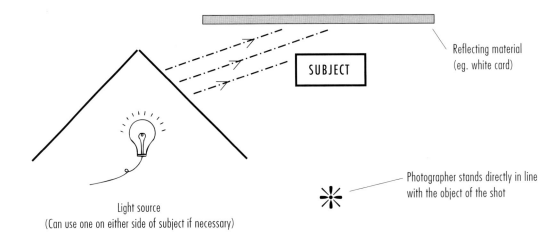

Reflecting material
(eg. white card)

SUBJECT

Photographer stands directly in line
with the object of the shot

Light source
(Can use one on either side of subject if necessary)

### HOW TO USE OBLIQUE LIGHT SOURCES FOR YOUR PHOTOGRAPHY

from beneath (see accompanying sketch). In our own case we have created a simple light table using a box with the base removed and replaced with slats. We pinned a large tracing paper sheet over the inverted box then placed a lamp beneath the box. Soft, diffused light filters through from beneath the work creating a remarkably effective image. Good results need not cost you the earth!

A shiny surface can be used as a homemade reflector to fill in shadows. Suitable materials include glossy white card and aluminium kitchen foil but any surfaces which will reflect light can be tried.

The neutral background you use for indoor work can be the same card or fabric you used outdoors. Alternatively, use a neutral wallpapered or painted wall, or use a bed sheet pinned to the wall. You could also experiment with shaded tone papers available from stationers. Another option is to paint your own backdrop. Permanently mounted roller blinds provides a selection of backgrounds at the pull of a blind cord and are particularly good for confined spaces as they roll out of the way very conveniently.

Supporting work indoors is often an irritating problem. One solution is to prepare a stand specifically for your photography. An economical option is to modify an existing easel, or make your own from the accompanying sketch plan opposite. The dimensions can be adjusted to suit the scale of your work. This makes an extremely versatile support for either vertical or horizontal shots. The

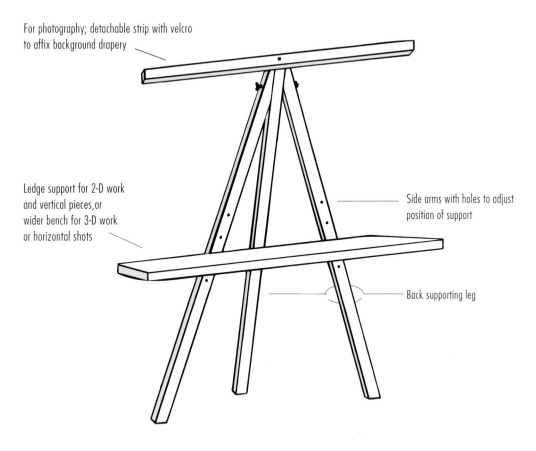

For photography; detachable strip with velcro to affix background drapery

Ledge support for 2-D work and vertical pieces, or wider bench for 3-D work or horizontal shots

Side arms with holes to adjust position of support

Back supporting leg

**SUPPORTING EASEL/STAND FOR PHOTOGRAPHING SMALL CRAFT/ART ITEMS**

time taken to make the easel will soon make up for the time spent fiddling with pieces to get the right angle or height to photograph your work.

The clear advantage of the indoor set up is that you have more control over the surroundings, although it may take a little experimentation to ascertain which methods work best.

### Conclusion

If you're not convinced that acquiring new skills and experiences can offer you interesting new directions, consider then that a blinkered approach which admits no distraction is not necessarily a 'safe' one. Survivors are those who successfully adapt to change. Remind yourself of this when you need to, and be prepared to widen your scope.

# MARKETING AND PROMOTION

*MARKETING CRAFT IS TOTALLY DIFFERENT to marketing a conventional High Street business. This goes some way to explaining why craft artists are generally so uncomfortable with and dismissive of conventional marketing methods. Successful marketing, however, is crucial to craft artists' survival so it's a matter of devising strategies that suit our particular needs.*

Unfortunately many craft artists do themselves poor service in their attitudes towards marketing. Unwillingness to take a professional approach towards retail clients is not intelligent behaviour—in practice it leads to retailers turning to cheap imports, not from personal taste or insensitivity to the quality of craft artists' work, but simply because of the frustrations in dealing with craft artists unprepared to be reliable, reasonable and realistic. Many craft artists we've talked to want people to buy their work, but felt it was inappropriate to sell their work. Their perceptions of marketing were typically jumbled—a confused image of soulless business executives engaged in dubious wheeler-dealing. Never were they short of justifications for steadfastly ignoring marketing principles: "if the work is good it will sell itself", "marketing is really for big business, it doesn't apply to me" and (complacently) "my work isn't commercial".

Our promise is that by focusing on marketing you will discover enhanced stimulus and freedom, and won't find your creativity hampered, as you might believe. By neglecting marketing there's more risk you'll become preoccupied with financial hardships. Your own marketing needn't be crass or in conflict with your artistic interests. It's possible to develop a unique style of marketing that won't compromise your integrity.

### Image

Being involved in creative work provides opportunities for you to express a distinctive image and style. This can either develop out of your work, or be planned. The image must be one that you are comfortable to be represented by. The 'look' of a craft artist venture should be very individual and you can coordinate the design of a logo, business cards, and other materials to strengthen the image.

### The fear of selling

We recently attended a marketing seminar entitled 'exposing your products to the risk of sale' which is an admirably terse summary of the marketing concept. Marketing texts and courses are often couched in language which can be off-putting to craft artists unfamiliar with the jargon. It's not a difficult or complex matter though, to grasp some of the keywords of the language. 'Marketing' for example, is not just another term for selling. Marketing takes account of the customer viewpoint as its centre. Taking the customer's needs into account is not as obvious as it may seem. It's easy to assume that what you want, is what your customer will want, but assumptions are often unwarranted. The 'marketing mix' is another expression that is bandied about. This is a description of the elements of the marketing process; the so-called four 'P's of marketing, which are:

- products (what you make)
- price
- promotion
- place (where your work is sold)

If you feel uncomfortable referring to what you create as a product, substitute 'my work' or another description if you prefer. 'Target marketing' is another common term. Essentially this means to discover what your customers have in common. Are your customers young, old, male, female, locals, tourists, and so on?

Bob and Ann Phillips' studio layout

*Craig Potton*

None of these terms are hard to comprehend. Marketing really boils down to common sense and a little thought. Some craft artists will find the going easier than others, but with a bit of effort, anyone can develop marketing abilities.

Our own experience offers a case in point because the attitudes we gently lampoon were once our own! Initially we scorned marketing ideas, but our gradual acceptance and adoption of advice meant that the message eventually got through. It's hard now to recall how sure we had been (on the basis of so little knowledge) of the irrelevance of marketing.

There are innumerable complex tomes on marketing, but for most craft artists a broad appreciation of the basics will do. Essentially you have two choices. Do you want to sell your work yourself, or do you want it sold on your behalf? There are arguments to support either option and you'll know your own feelings and circumstances best. You may not trust another to convey the intentions expressed in your work, or perhaps you want your clients to see your work in its context, in its own environment.

## DIY: SELLING YOUR OWN WORK—STUDIOS, EXHIBITIONS, ART SHOWS

There are many ways to sell your work yourself: from your own studio (either regularly or intermittently); from retail space shared with other craft artists; from exhibitions or art and craft shows.

### Selling from a studio

Selling direct from a studio has the advantage that the returns from your work are higher because there are no commission or wholesale discounts to be paid. When selling from a home studio it's a good idea to keep a separate entrance for your studio if possible, otherwise people can feel uncomfortable about 'invading your home'. This won't apply to an occasional 'open day' as your customers are invited, and the 'at home' atmosphere is acceptably personal.

Appearances are important and however untidy you may be naturally, try to keep the entrance and studio area looking clean and attractive. This ensures that a customer's first impression on arrival is positive. Signs should be attractive, your work should be well presented and maintained. Display considerations are vitally important to marketing your work. We all have different ideas on display and layout of our studio and whilst displays shouldn't be cluttered with little tags everywhere, make sure your customers can clearly see the prices otherwise they may be discouraged from taking a closer interest.

Those who find this method of marketing works well tend to be at either end of the spectrum. Those part-time craft artists who are happy to make a supplementary income from their work and can do so on a fairly small clientele often start here, and then expand to combine other methods of marketing such as wholesaling as their income needs demand. This approach also works particularly well for high profile craft artists who are producing highly priced individual works. They too, are in a position to derive their living from a small number of customers who collect their work and actively seek such artists out.

Against this approach you should consider the likely intrusions into your private life, and the extra demands that may be made on your time. Even where opening hours are posted the public can be overly demanding. If you advertise set opening hours then stick to them; if your timekeeping is erratic this gives a bad impression. Better to cut down to hours you can cope with more easily if it's a problem. Satisfaction with this approach often depends on individual preferences. We enjoy meeting our customers and several have become close friends over the years. The main drawback is the considerable time spent talking to visitors which puts pressure on your ability to work and remain solvent.

A good compromise for those who really need time to get on with work 'proper' and still make sales, is to strictly limit the times that you open. One artist we know has this down to a fine art, just running a few 'open home' days during the year. This is probably too extreme unless you are happy to sell a small quantity of work from time to time. Opening only at weekends could be a useful compromise to limit the time you make yourself available. You may then try to take a day off midweek, but it doesn't always work out! It may require trial and error, but with thought you'll to strike a balance that suits. If you live in a popular tourist area you may want to concentrate your marketing efforts so that you open during the season, then close in the off season.

The craft artist whose entire livelihood is derived working from a home studio/workshop has to learn the art of saying "no". We're usually delighted to

**SHOP HOURS**

OPEN Most Days About 9 or 10
Occasionally as Early as 7, But SOME DAYS
As Late As 12 or 1.
WE CLOSE About 5:30 or 6
Occasionally About 4 or 5, But
Sometimes as Late as 11 or 12.
SOME DAYS OR Afternoons, We
Aren't Here At All, and Lately
I've Been Here Just About All The Time,
Except When I'm Someplace Else,
But I Should Be Here Then, Too.

*Photo: Craig Potton*

show groups and individuals around, but by appointment and only at the times we nominate. This approach wasn't easy to implement and in the first couple of years our work was disrupted because folk arrived unannounced until we amended the situation. Setting a time that suits you, or putting on an occasional open day may ensure a sane blend of PR and quiet time.

Getting together with other craft artists working from studios in your area to coordinate marketing can work very well. Business people have the networking help of the 'old boy' system, chambers of commerce and the like—craft artists can use networks to advantage too! Where we live there is a concentration of craft artists working in a variety of media (glass, pottery, painting, weaving etc) and by cooperating we can target visitors with a strong interest in art and crafts. It may be possible to establish similar networks in your area. By supporting one another you attract more customers to your home workshop/studio than you'd be able to manage by operating in isolation.

A hint: when setting up a home studio it's important that your customers are encouraged to make purchases without feeling they are interrupting your work. Some craft artists install a buzzer or a bell for customers who require attention, others have another person (often a spouse or an employee) to attend to customers. All our craft artist colleagues confirmed the need to talk to your studio visitors. This comes as an effort if you're reserved by nature. Don't worry that you're 'not a salesman'. Remember that salesmen in regular business have to work hard to achieve product knowledge and enthusiasm. You already have a

headstart! Keep in mind that people want to talk to you, not to some hard-selling alter ego. Be natural and you'll find it gets easier and more enjoyable with time.

There is a down side to working alone from home or studio. We have spoken to several craft artists who experienced such difficulties in trying to do everything alone that they now advise against similar attempts. The problem lies in putting aside time for creative work. Even those who comfortably work to a crowd found that the constant distractions and interruptions from visitors made working creatively and productively difficult.

Estuary Arts Gallery

*Craig Potton*

### Exhibitions

Staging an exhibition attracts customers and secures recognition for you and your work. An exhibition also attracts those customers who lack confidence in their opinions and feel reassured about their purchases when buying from an established gallery.

Exhibitions vary in size and prestige from a display in your local library to a national event. With the latter, considerable effort and expense is involved. Portfolios will be demanded and your work may be out of circulation for months. Sole exhibitions can boost sales dramatically. The openings often feature a 'meet the craft artist' theme. People respond well to this format, especially if you talk interestingly and informatively about your exhibited work. This gives a special personal relevance to the customer's purchase and provides an experience they can talk about with their friends. This in turn can lead to greater recognition for you and higher sales. In marketing terms you've effectively given the customer 'added value' with the piece they've bought from you. The work is a conversation piece and has a higher personal worth in the client's eyes because they've met the creator of the work.

Entering your work in exhibitions combines well with other marketing avenues. You might for example sell from your own studio, but exhibit to raise your profile or to secure sales in another area. Some craft artists depend entirely on exhibitions for sales of their work, and certainly for those of established reputation, exhibiting may be the only marketing approach employed. Invariably this state of affairs has been created through considerable effort over many years in which the craft artist has employed one or several of the other methods of marketing in order to attain such a happy position! Again, for the person who is not entirely dependent upon sales for a livelihood, exhibitions may provide all the sales desired. Some are delighted to sell just a few pieces of work each year, and for these craft artists exhibiting is a pleasurable and effective way of achieving their aim. It all hinges on what you want to achieve.

Bear in mind too, that if you don't feel that a gallery is the right context there are many other places other than the conventional gallery where you could exhibit: airport lounges, shopping malls, civic buildings, libraries…the list of choices depends on you and on the opportunities in your area.

With some exhibitions, particularly in well-known galleries, the associated costs can be high, so it's a good idea to establish who meets what costs. The advertising and promotional costs, catering for exhibition opening gatherings, display materials and other expenses should be clearly understood, not just the commission that the gallery deducts from the retail price of your work. All arrangements, from packing and shipping to insurance cover should ideally be agreed upon before the exhibition takes place. Some galleries will have a standard guide sheet which sets the ground rules. If they don't, then a letter which details the terms and conditions will reduce the chance of misunderstandings.

Pricing your work should be discussed openly with the gallery owner if you are unsure what level to set your prices. Extravagant price tags may impress, but unless you're reasonably famous or fortunate, you'll be wise to ensure that your work is reasonably priced. This way it ends up in other people's appreciative homes, rather than back in your own! This is not to say that high ticket prices aren't possible, just that they're easier to pull off with an established reputation. If you haven't scaled those dizzy heights yet, then demanding breathtaking prices will just ensure a cluttered home! (We offer more advice on pricing your work in chapter 7)

Checking the art/craft grapevine could point you in the right direction when it comes to finding a suitable venue for a solo exhibition. If you've been invited to exhibit don't be too flattered to check with other craftspeople on their dealings with the gallery concerned. Although rip-offs are extremely rare we do hear stories of sell-out exhibitions where the artist has had to fight tooth and nail for the money to be paid out (which is difficult if you live a long way away from the offending gallery).

These (rare) problems aside, in practically all cases exhibiting your work will be a positive experience and provide you with a range of benefits: valuable criticism of your work, an appreciation of standards both of work and of display, and exposure of your best work to a receptive public, some of whom may become loyal customers. Do what you can to ensure they do!

Gallery owners almost invariably maintain customer lists of potential buyers. An exhibition will enable you to start a similar list of people who have taken a positive interest in your work. You can build records of your good customers into a vital marketing tool. By maintaining contact with your customers and making them feel special, then you'll very likely sell to them again…and again. Collectors frequently start in a small way. Look after good customers, keep them in touch with new achievements and new work. If you are exhibiting work in their area send them an invitation to the opening. Like the gallery owner you now have a collection of names of potential customers to form the basis of invitation lists for future exhibitions.

Finally, a word on criticism. Some craft artists are totally demoralised by the criticisms of their work during the selection process or at the exhibition. Try not to be affected in this way. All judging is subjective to some degree and if you're nursing a rejection or if you're smarting from bad reviews take heart and remember that the same piece at a different time and place could earn a totally different appraisal! Accept valid commentary with grace, but don't take anything else to heart! In this spirit, you will find exhibitions both rewarding and stimulating.

## Craft fairs and art shows

We cannot stress too strongly that if you're considering selling your work through art/craft shows you *must* find the fair or show that is appropriate for your work. A good fair or show offers the opportunity to gain public reaction to your work. Choosing suitable events is vital because you risk damaging your reputation for quality by becoming involved with any bazaars or fleamarket operations which

Craft exhibit                                                                                         *Simon Field*

includes sellers of mass-produced products. Where possible visit the show you are considering before applying. You may be judged by the company you keep so ensure that your work fits comfortably with the selling environment.

Some areas operate regular indoor or outdoor art/craft events. Don't automatically rule out the outdoor shows; some of them are well-run prestigious affairs attracting a high standard of exhibitor and a discerning clientele. These outdoor shows often have standard covered stalls or booths within a large marquee (or a series of marquees for the larger shows). Some will be held at fixed times or seasons of the year, such as Easter or spring.

Shows on offer range from local community fairs to highly organised national events. The best of them bring you into direct contact with a large number of potential customers in a short period and allow you to gauge their response to your work, ie to carry out your market research.

We have been involved with both national craft fairs and overseas shows and find that for us they fulfill a number of important functions. The show format means that the craft artist retains total control in creating, displaying and selling to the customer. As well, this avenue offers tremendous social contacts with craftspeople from different places and establishes a friendly network over a large area. Often this network is a valuable link for support; we've often fielded calls to check on the reliability of suppliers or buyers. Effective market research is perhaps the major advantage for the new craft artist. At large well-promoted shows the numbers visiting your booth are such that one can readily check reaction to your work first hand.

The customers who attend shows are not all gallery regulars and so under normal circumstances may not have the opportunity to admire your work. Many enjoy the friendly environment and save their gift buying for the annual appearance of the show in their city. For the craft artist starting out, these shows will bring exposure to customers who are already interested in craft and art. For the artist working in isolation they bring much needed contact with other craft artists as well as with clients. Larger established fairs and interior design-type shows also have the potential to attract clients for major orders and commissions.

The costs involved can be substantial. A small local fair will probably offer booths for a small donation, but large, professionally run craft shows offer greater rewards, with accordingly higher costs.

Most professionally operated shows require a portfolio to be submitted. Applications have to be well presented if they are even to be considered. The illustrations show typical requirements for submitted slides. Increasingly exhibitors have professionally taken sets to enhance their chance of entry into their chosen shows. The important issue of photographing art and craft work is covered in the previous chapter. Is it all worth it? Well it's a case of 'you pays your money and you takes your choice'—except that in this case it's the selectors' choice! And just how much do you pay if you're one of the chosen

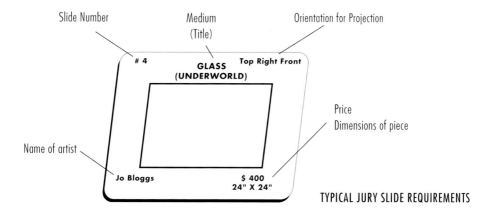

TYPICAL JURY SLIDE REQUIREMENTS

few? There are wide variations but for the good shows, fees can be more than $500 for a site. For their part, good shows offer the exhibitor an attractive deal. Prize money can run into many thousands, professional, high-budget promotion is carried out, and these shows do attract buyers (some of whom become loyal collectors who come every year to shows, travelling long distances if necessary). The very fact there is keen competition to enter these shows speaks volumes for the argument that these shows DO deliver!

## SELLING TO GALLERIES AND SHOPS

Selling to galleries and shops is either done on a wholesale basis, where the retailer buys work from you, or on consignment, where you are paid when your work sells. In either case a personal visit to the outlet, shop or gallery is a good idea. Check that your work will fit comfortably with the other work being sold there. Treat your potential retailer with courtesy. Make an appointment with the owner or manager (there is no point dealing with staff with no power to purchase) and go to the appointment prepared to discuss your work in an open, confident way. Faith in your work should be easy! Listen to the response you get. People really hate to turn you down and if your work doesn't fit with their outlet they are usually happy to suggest another contact to try. Good backup material is invaluable. Some craftspeople have a sample collection of their work ready to show to retailers, others use photographic illustrations particularly if the pieces are large and not so easily toted around in a sample case! Brochures are often the first introduction potential customers have to you and the work you do, so it's vital that they do a good job for you. Because brochures and business cards are so important they will be covered separately in the following section on promotion.

Compared with consignment arrangements, where the craftsperson takes all the risk, in wholesaling the retailer buys your work and takes the risk that it will re-sell readily. This is a welcome state of affairs for the craft artist but there are compromises to be made. In recognition that the shop may have to wait some time before selling the work, and thereby earning the profit which provides the

Art of Living Gallery

*Craig Potton*

retailer's livelihood, wholesaled goods normally give you a lower return than consigned pieces (on the plus side you get your money quicker).

It's tempting to bemoan the size of retail mark-ups. Remember, however, that while waiting for your work to sell, the retailer still has to pay shop leases, wages, insurance, and other overheads. Bear in mind too that the retailer may spend hours discussing your work with customers without making a sale. Such discussions prepare the ground for future sales, though not necessarily through that outlet. Any referral that a gallery or other outlet provides you with should be acknowledged out of courtesy. Depending on the value, a commission payment could be appropriate too, recognising the work done on your behalf.

Selling through shops and galleries rules out a significant measure of control over the way your work is presented by a retailer. Nevertheless, since they have usually committed their own money to the outlet's operation, retailers have a good incentive to display your work well and promote sales. If you have helpful ideas for display and promotion of your work discuss them (tactfully) with the retailer.

Marketing work to shops or galleries, or selling through agents, has the advantage of leaving the craft artist freer to concentrate on what they do best. Consigning your work can be riskier and less lucrative than wholesaling. Far more paperwork is involved too, always a cogent argument against! In fairness to the consignment sales approach, high priced items have a smaller market and few outlets are willing (or able) to buy outright unless the craft artist has a well-established track record.

When consigning your work, and without being unduly pessimistic, it is a good idea to ensure that the work is clearly identifiable and that you retain documentation and preferably photographs too. At least one craft artist of our acquaintance has lost work, so ensure that you keep good records and can identify any work left on consignment unequivocally! In cases of galleries with financial woes, many craftspeople have lost stock or at least had to wait months before their work was returned. If the craft artists' grapevine issues advance warning of a gallery foundering, act promptly to recover your work. Leave it too long and it may be a long, frustrating time before you see it again, if ever!

Still on things negative, it's increasingly common for shops to establish with small amounts of capital and rely on having all, or nearly all stock on consignment. The decision whether or not to leave work on consignment is an individual one. A trial period is a good compromise. If the retailer sells your stock and sends you a regular monthly cheque then you need have no qualms about the arrangement. Again, the reputation of some shops and galleries may be so high that just having your work on display in them is prestigious—certainly worth consigning stock there even if it's not your normal preference.

New craft artists may have to leave work on consignment even in less prestigious stores. Ensure that the shop does its part by maintaining your stock in good condition and paying at the agreed times as the work sells. With distant outlets this is very hard to control. Unless you have a contact in the area, you won't know when your work has sold. Unfortunately it's common for shop leases, overdrafts and other bills to have priority over the craft artist's cheque. A trial period on both sides can be diplomatically offered, after all the retailer has to know if your work is saleable too! With new stores a trial period will give you a chance to see how well you're going to work together. You'll soon know whether it's worth continuing the relationship.

For your part look after your good outlets as you would any good customer. Keep stock supplied, fill orders promptly, don't undercut a local outlet if you have your own studio showroom, and generally treat them as you'd expect to be treated were you on the other side of the counter. You might consider offering them exclusivity or other benefits as appropriate. Steady and reliable outlets will sustain you between those big cheques for the 'masterpieces' that sometimes take forever to sell!

Retailers and craft artists need not take up an 'us and them' stance. Our goals and attitudes are surprisingly compatible, and it's possible to forge a lasting and mutually advantageous relationship!

## AGENTS

Why use agents to market your work? Situations where agent representation is valuable arise if you live in an isolated area and it's uneconomic to travel to visit your outlets. An agent will usually represent a number of craft artists so costs are spread. Provided that the other agencies fit in

There are many opportunities for craft artists to secure work for awards and presentations. Here Air New Zealand executive Irene King discusses a selection of presentation pieces with Bob.

*Ann Phillips*

well with your work, an agent can promote and sell your work effectively.

When looking for an agent/sales representative, or when approached by one looking to add more agencies to his list, consult the craft artists' grapevine. It helps to know what other types of agencies the agent holds, and how many! If you have difficulty in locating an agent it is a good idea to ask buyers in outlets similar to those you hope to sell to for a recommendation. Agents should convince you of their interest in your work, otherwise they're unlikely to sell your work well.

There are standard terms of agreement for agent representatives, including such details as the duration of the agreement, commission rates, when payments are to be made, and conditions under which the agreement could be terminated. A trial period is an excellent idea. Bear in mind that there may be different rates for different lines, for example if an agent is handling domestic and gallery work. Differential rates can be worked out on an individual basis. A useful tip from an agent-weary craft artist is to have an agreement for a set trial period. No more than a few months at first, to find out if the arrangement is going to work out. After the trial period, and if the arrangement is satisfactory to both sides, the agreement would then be made for a longer term. Provision should also be made to allow either party to terminate the agreement with an appropriate period of notice—usually at least a month. A clear, unambiguous agreement will enable you to avoid frustrating misunderstandings.

## MARKETING: THE COOPERATIVE APPROACH

Craft artists who combine forces to share the selling of work are in a much stronger position than those operating from their own studio. Those we know in cooperatives are generally very positive about this method of marketing their work because:

- time and cost commitments are shared
- sales and marketing efforts can be strengthened
- a wider range of craft can be offered to visitors
- better locations can be secured to offer your work to the public

## COMMISSION AND CONTRACT WORK

Compared with other marketing methods, working to a particular contract or commission is fairly unpredictable. A craft artist might go for years without a commission then secure three in as many months! Large public contracts can be rewarding both financially and in terms of building your reputation. One major contract can lead to several more, particularly when other similar projects are being planned. Frequently the same project advisors (usually interior designers or architects, depending on the type of project) are used and having worked with you before, could well approach you with more work!

A commission is a marvellous opportunity and perhaps the only chance you'll get to work on a grand scale, or to execute work that will be the making of your reputation as a fine craft artist.

The down side is that sometimes things don't go at all well. In the euphoria of securing a magnificent commission dotting the 'i's and crossing the 't's can be overlooked. With any commission clear written agreements are necessary (not always easy to insist upon though, particularly if this is your first major project and you're flattered and excited). There are exceptions of course, if, for example, you're so enthralled with the project that you'd feel honoured to do the work for free, fine. If not, then get that piece of paper! Once you have that, you can go back to being the artist and ignore the business detail if that's your preferred stance!

On a less lavish scale there are still many opportunities to secure contract work for awards, trophies and general presentations. This line of marketing could be equally helpful in your career. Ideas that other craft artists have put to good use include creating presentations for conferences, for sports organisations, service groups and businesses.

## CONCLUSION

No matter what genre of craft or art your efforts represent, and no matter at what level of involvement you find yourself, there are tremendous benefits in evaluating how best to market your work. Some of the foregoing hints, tips and cautionary tales may already strike a chord with you! By now we trust that you have a clearer picture of where you want to go with your art or craft. Re-evaluate your position regularly, and stay alert to new openings and novel ideas. The important thing is to develop as you want to. There's little point following some idealised success model that works for others if it doesn't fit your particular needs (no matter how weird others may consider them).

The key to success with many craft enterprises has been to simply find what makes the particular venture special. How it differs from similar ventures, what sets it apart. If you can start to answer such queries about your own aims and what makes your work unique, then marketing skills will come easily!

## TELLING THE REST OF
## THE WORLD ABOUT YOU
## ... PROMOTION

In order to appreciate the work that you do others must be made aware of its existence! Unless you are blessed with your own fairy godmother it is highly unlikely that you will benefit from sitting on your talent, waiting to be discovered! Daydreams aside, the odds of being discovered by a grateful and appreciative world are not high. If on the other hand you're prepared to bring your creative work to the attention of others, then not only do you enhance public recognition of your work, you also encourage appreciation of quality craft art in general. Promotion is not defined as an excuse to indulge your ego, but rather a way to inform interested people about creative work they can relate to and value. To introduce work of unique quality instilled with the feeling and ability of the craft artist who created it (you), is surely a worthy aim!

## SELF-PROMOTION
## USING THE MEDIA

Promotion and marketing are closely linked. Self-promotion is often the best way to awaken potential clients to the fact of your existence. A simple first step is to contact the media with an idea. Here, from a freelance journalist are some 'insider' tips. Don't say "there is no interest in art and craft" at the first rebuff, but think how you could re-present the item with a different, more newsworthy slant and therefore be published. Read papers and magazines to get a feel for their style. Perseverance will usually be rewarded. In general what makes items newsworthy is a sufficiently strong human interest angle. It takes a little nous to apply this to your own situation and in some cases the news angle you come up with may seem a long way from the art and crafts scene directly. For example, if there is a high level of unemployment in your area, the craft artist as employer would be a promising slant. If you've taken on an apprentice under a training incentive scheme, then this sort of positive news should be welcomed for publication. True, it may not be specifically about your work but you'll be publicised in a very positive light because of the employment/human interest angle! This is just one example. Check local publications circulating in your area and evaluate the angles that secured a place in them for news stories or features.

### The craft artist as advocate

Generating interest in crafts generally, rather than just in your own work, is very important. Perhaps a group you are involved in is organising an exhibition. Tell others about it. Local newspapers, radio, and television stations are always on the lookout for interesting community events. See what other craft artists do for promotion. Have you or other craftspeople carried out a major commission recently, or had interesting visiting craft artists present workshops. All of these can be of wide general interest and will raise the level of awareness of creative happenings in the community.

## BROCHURES

A carefully designed brochure about you and your work is a common promotional tool. These can range from an inexpensive brochure card to a costly foldout presentation. Your aim is to ensure maximum impact and this requires thoughtful planning. Remember that these promotional materials will often be your sole representative and a customer may decide to seek you out on the basis of the impression they have gained.

Begin your brochure by drafting out a few alternatives then seek constructive criticism from those whose opinions you value and who can be relied upon for a candid response. If you seek professional help from a graphic designer, it's important to make sure the style reflects your work. Consider the impression of your work that you want to convey—a brash supermarket style promotion tool will not strike the right note if you want to project a restrained, high-quality gallery image.

Check the basics, ensuring your name is prominent at the top and all details of contact address and opening hours are accurate. Include in your brochure a good pictorial representation of your work, a summary of your background

Detail of ceramic piece by
Christine Boswijk
*Julia Brooke-White*

(CV), a guide to your work stressing what sets it apart, any awards and important commissions. Keep the 'artist statement' of your personal approach, philosophy and influences, brief. With any writing for publication it's always a good idea to ask someone else with English skills to read over your text to check for spelling mistakes, incorrect grammar or poor sentence construction.

Transferring your ideas to the finished printed product requires the help of either a graphic designer or a desktop publishing bureau. Graphic designers are more expensive but are well worthwhile if you are planning a high-quality brochure using colour photography. For more straightforward brochures you can ask a desktop publishing bureau to computer typeset the brochure layout working from a mockup and text prepared by you. Always carefully proofread any typesetting to make sure all the text you have supplied has been set, and to check for any spelling or typographical errors that may have arisen. Both graphic designers and desktop publishing bureaux can offer advice on printers and arrange for competitive printing quotes.

For special exhibitions you may require a separate brochure, professional portfolio and/or exhibition catalogue. The same information should be included in these publications and a photo of yourself is normally included. Again, aim for high visual appeal, after all, how much of the 'bumpf' from promotional material do you ever retain? Aside from your nearest and dearest most don't look beyond the pictures and name!

## ADVERTISING

The advertising possibilities will depend on what is available to you in your area, but certainly don't feel you 'can't play' without a big advertising budget. Work out what you want to do and what you can afford—present this to the advertising staff of the chosen media and see what sort of deal they can put together for you. If you are opening in a new area for example, an advertising feature page in the local newspaper (usually tied to advertisements of associated craft artists) is one way of securing good promotion of your new venture for a modest outlay.

Most craft artists get by with an occasional special advertisement perhaps publicising a special event such as a studio open day. Another occasion craft artists use to advertise is when an exhibition is being staged and promotion costs are shared with the gallery.

Fish painting on silk by Jenny Barraud
*Craig Potton*

## *Putting an advert together*

When faced with a blank sheet of paper those of us not gifted with copywriting ability spend a lot of time pencil gnawing. Help is at hand from the staff of the advertising medium concerned. Thus the local newspaper or radio should be able to help you put together effective copy. For example, the craft artist on a tight budget is tempted to squeeze a lot into their 'ad' but fewer words, well set out, carry more impact than a lot of verbiage crammed into a small space. In a sea of closely spaced newsprint, blank areas attract the eye. Advertisers can use the gaps around the print, termed 'white space' to good effect.

Collaborating with other craft artists can result in cost-effective advertising for a special event. A group of craft artists we know decided to contribute to an advertising kitty to be spent on newspaper advertisements telling the public that their studios would be thrown open for one day. First they checked the local newspapers to ensure their distribution covered the area. Next they analysed which adverts attracted attention and why. One gambit they liked was the advertisement of a special or limited opportunity. They noted that potters publicise kiln opening days, and came up with the idea of promoting a unique opportunity to view studios normally unseen. The open day was well supported by the public and has since grown to become an annual open weekend!

## PUBLIC SPEAKING

A fact of life for many craft artists is that they are simply not in a position to come up with attractive brochures or advertising to generate public interest in their work. Constructive and effective publicity at negligible or no cost can still be achieved by careful use of the media (see page 59) or through indirect promotion methods such as public speaking. To support a particular exhibition in a gallery or museum, craft artists may be invited to talk about their work. In a more general public arena organisations are always on the lookout for interesting guests who can talk about their special subject. Your local art group could encourage members to tell each other about their own particular interests. Once comfortable giving a talk or slide show to a small group of familiar faces you are better prepared for the progression to talking to larger associations.

Learn the knack of fitting a talk to the audience. Having sat through tedious lectures, totally inappropriate for the audience, we always try to pitch our talk to the particular group. One spiel for all won't do! Audience size shouldn't faze you. Talking to 100 people is no harder than talking to 10 …it can be easier if there are lots of questions! Recently we were invited to speak to a women's group (normally an informal gathering of 20 or so). On arrival on the appointed day we found the large carpark full, so assumed another function was on. Walking inside we faced a packed hall of several hundred women! All went well but there was an interesting sequel. We watched the evening news on television that night and noted with glee that the Prime Minister addressing a local meeting had attracted only 38!

Whatever audience size you face, you are almost certain to attract new clients. There's a strong personal element in buying craft and art and 'getting to know' the artist enhances sales of your work. How you tackle the actual talk will depend on your personal inclinations. We keep our talks light and chatty with humour as an icebreaker to establish a rapport. You may like to illustrate your talk with slides (just a few), or with examples of your work. You might even have work for sale at the conclusion of the talk. This could be the ideal psychological time to sell to a receptive public! (Toting a visa machine may be bordering on the tacky though … one for the bolder craft artist to try perhaps.)

## RADIO AND TELEVISION

Radio and TV advertising is expensive and craft artists rarely use this method of promotion. There are always exceptions though. Community radio stations sometimes offer inexpensive packages which will help attract new clients and encourage back existing ones. Craft cooperatives (having a group budget rather than an individual pocket) have often made good use of local radio, and in some cases local television.

Artist Nicola Mannering
painting ceramic tiles.
*Craig Potton*

## CONCLUSION

These are just some of the promotional approaches you might take.
Depending on your strengths, inclinations and circumstances your means
of promotion can range from well designed cards right through to a home page
on the Internet! All the better if you can secure free promotion but remember
there are rarely free lunches in life and what you will need to devise is a
promotional strategy that gives you good value for your investment. Try to be
consistent so that all forms of promotion reinforce the view of your work that
you want to communicate. It will take you time and effort to devise a strategy
but you can do it.

   The concept of promotion sits uneasily with many craft artists, but without
promotion there is little chance of potential buyers becoming acquainted with
your work. Like marketing, promotion doesn't have to be crass or expensive.
Rather, promotion can be accomplished in ways that suit your needs, style and
budget. It doesn't necessarily mean aiming to attract mass market interest—
indeed there are those who require just a few people to regularly buy their work
in order to be sustained for life.

# PLAYING
# THE
# MONEY GAME

*We shall look first at the need for finance, and some angles on avoiding overdrafts before considering how to prepare a good case when seeking financial help.*

## MONEY PROBLEMS

**F**irst, accept that money shortage is not unique to the 'struggling artist'. In even the largest corporate enterprise there are fluctuations in income. Understand this and see that the craft artist needing short term overdrafts to buffer fluctuations in money supply is just practising what big business does, but on a much smaller scale!

## MONEY WITHOUT BORROWING

**W**hile extra finance is usually required in an establishment phase, it's worth bearing in mind that not all cash shortages that occur automatically mean that you need to borrow. Adjusting the way you run your enterprise can sometimes make up the shortfall. A printmaker colleague who had been enjoying excellent sales recently, noticed that despite this, he was often overdrawn and he was paying high bank fees. Though an unenthusiastic bookkeeper, he found by putting in more effort here, (specifically, sending out invoices promptly and chasing up overdue payments) his account was soon in the black, bank fees dropped dramatically and the cash shortage problem was resolved.

Another area of your venture to review during a cash shortage is whether or not your prices are too low to be profitable. Check your pricing if you suspect this could be the weak point in your cost structure. Make sure that your costs haven't crept up without prices taking account of them, as well as considering ways to reduce your costs.

Looking at these options may involve you in a little thinking and calculating, but as craft artists we are meant to be creative! A surprising number have found a solution to a cash shortage without having to borrow.

## BORROWING

In the absence of a convenient fairy godmother it's highly likely you'll need to look around for a source of outside financing, even if only as a short term measure. If you don't have sufficient funds of your own (and chances are you won't) consider all available options.

In many cases there are special assistance packages or low interest loans available for new creative enterprises in your region. There may be special grants available to artists and craftspeople, or community funded low-rent workshops and galleries. It makes good sense to explore all these options first, after all, the conditions and repayment terms are much more favourable than from your conventional lending institutions! Check that the conditions suit you; for example where low-rent workspace is provided you may have to be present during core work hours and provide public demonstrations. Your own local arts organisations and citizens advice bureaux will be able to advise on what is available within your area. This sort of specialised help could provide a tremendous boost for you.

We know of a case where a young sculptor of some years experience, who was gradually establishing a name for himself, had been repeatedly refused start-up finance for his own workshop/studio. His only available option was to join in a community work-space. Several years on he is doing well, and in fact enjoys the group working environment so much that he has adjusted his initial dream of acquiring his own space. Despite having changed his ambition he finds he could now have it, if he wanted to. His bank statements frequently come with enclosed circulars encouraging him to apply for the bank's competitive loan finance! This seems to support the truth of the adage that 'bankers don't lend you money unless you can prove you don't need it'.

## BANKS

If you have to approach a bank or other mainstream lending institution for money, the following tips, gleaned from both successful and fruitless encounters between craftspeople and lenders, may help.

Essentially you are trying to persuade another person (who may know nothing of your work and care even less) that you are a 'safe risk', that you have a valid use for the money, and that there are sufficiently good prospects for repayment to be expected. Success in applying for a bank loan often depends on establishing a feeling of confidence. You must be sure of your ability to make a go of the project you're seeking finance for and radiate this confidence! The lender should then (hopefully) be inspired with a similar confidence in you.

At the weaving loom.
*Birgite Armstrong International Weaving School of New Zealand*

### Presenting your case

Friends who have succeeded in raising finance to set up or to develop their enterprise found that it was often important to 'play the game' with a lender, by which we mean adopting a fairly conventional approach (for some this extended to modifying their personal appearance!). Figures and plans are needed of course, but the way they are presented is at least as important!

A good example of this was a weaver who was given a loan on the identical written proposal that was rejected several months earlier by the same institution. In the interval she'd had her application neatly typed and bound in a professional looking folder, invested in a 'power haircut' and padded-shoulder suit, and generally tried to fit the mould. She maintains that just looking the part tipped the balance. Her interviewer didn't recognise her, and dealt with her in a totally different way. Maybe it was the look, or maybe the first interview made her better prepared to put her case. In fact it is a smart move to get in a little practice before the all-important application interview. Have a friend play devil's advocate with some awkward questions. It may seem a bit of a joke at the time, but when the real target throws these at you at the interview, you've had a chance to sort out a tactical response! Practising fielding indifferent or hostile queries might help you fly through the loan application with ease.

Written project proposals must be well presented and you should be completely familiar with the material that you are submitting. One craft artist who wanted to increase his overdraft facilities had an accountant draw up an impressive feasibility study to support his application. Unwisely he went in "clutching this document, none of which I understood well enough to field questions about!" After an ignominious rebuff he did his homework and eventually secured his overdraft. Which goes to show that nothing promotes self-confidence more than knowing what you're talking about!

### Other options

Borrowing may be the obvious approach, but it is not the only way of securing what you want. Hire purchase and/or credit facilities could be worth considering if you need funding to buy or upgrade equipment, perhaps a new kiln or a table loom. The advantage is that you don't have to front up with all the money at once, so you are spared a large capital outlay, which at the time might be impossible.

For many craft artists a short-term overdraft facility to tide over periods of income fluctuation is all that is required. This will enable you to cope with such common irregularities as delays in being paid for work supplied to shops or galleries, seasonal fluctuations (like those experienced by tourist-orientated enterprises) and large outgoings, such as those you might incur when you invest in raw materials.

If you record the fluctuations that occur in your venture and talk to your bank manager well before the time you need an overdraft, then often arranging such a facility is an easy formality. The benefit of the arrangement for you is that you are only paying interest on the exact amount of money that you need, and for the period of time that you need it. The bank provides outside support only when you need it, and you pay for this as and when you use it. This can be a cheaper option than a fixed loan. As our example demonstrated, it's very hard to put your case if you don't understand the information supporting it.

### A business plan - getting it down on paper

When you apply for financial help you will need to present a clear overview of your enterprise. This is called a business plan, essentially an objective summary of what you are up to!

It outlines what you do, what you make, where your income comes from. More than this though, it puts your ambitions down on paper, your prospects, your short term and longer term goals, what you would like to see happen in the next five years. It should certainly include your particular strengths, but opinion is divided on the wisdom of including your weak areas. If you point out your weaknesses, highlight your positive moves to offset them!

Because a business plan will be required to support any funding application that you make, it will have to include a financial summary. Try not to go overboard producing a mass of figures. Balance quality with quantity! It is easy to churn out impressive looking tables and graphs on a computer, but any conclusions drawn need to be supported!

Basic financial data normally presented are:

- Balance sheet—data on the current state of your enterprise (what is happening now, what you owe and what you are owed)
- Profit and Loss—data on the history of your enterprise (what has already happened)

Textile artist Jenny Barraud

*Craig Potton*

- A regular tally of income and expenditure. (Keep this for yourself to keep on top of what is happening through the year, rather than waiting for the books to be 'done' to find out).
- Cash flow statement—data on the future of your enterprise (what should happen). This shows you when you spend and when you make. It is useful for seeing when seasonal fluctuations occur so that overdrafts can be arranged in advance.

The first thing (cynics might say the only thing) in your business plan that is read is the summary, so ensure first impressions are good! Your enthusiasm should surface here, a positive approach can only do your application good (as long as it is supported by the hard information). A well written, positive summary, together with a confident presentation can often tip the balance in your favour when the bank makes its decision. This doesn't mean that you should gloss over problems, but anticipate reservations and show that you can deal with ups and downs. You need to convey the belief that the investment is a good one. Realistic optimism is probably the line to aim for.

If the answer is no, then examine the criticisms or given reasons for denying your application. If they seem reasonable and fair then do your homework and present a better case next time. If you feel unfairly treated you can complain and challenge the decision. Ultimately though, you may have to change banks and work on developing a better relationship with your new bank manager.

If your venture is relatively new, or not yet begun, the business plan or proposal may be called a feasibility study. In a feasibility study you anticipate the future of your venture in order to evaluate your ideas. Preparing the financial data will probably involve experienced help, especially if it's breaking new ground for you. Ask your advisors to explain what they have done and to go over the main points with you. Ensure you understand everything and next year you might be confident enough to go it alone!

As well as providing you with a necessary backup when you are looking for funds, a business plan is invaluable because it makes you sort out just what you and your enterprise are about. Having to commit pen to paper will force you to look hard at what you're doing and see how close to your earliest ambitions you are staying! The plan summarises what is happening and that in itself often suggests new options to explore.

# CHAPTER 7

# HOW MUCH? —PRICING YOUR WORK

*THE MOST BASIC EXCHANGE that a craft artist has with the outside world is when he or she offers their work for sale. As craft artists we should expect a fair recompense for our experience, skill and creativity—in other words a decent living from our work. As we discussed in chapter one, this is something each craft artist must determine for his or her own circumstances.*

# PRODUCTION PIECES—
# WORKING OUT A WHOLESALE PRICE

**M**any craft artists have two disparate valuations to consider. First their 'bread and butter items' and second their 'unique pieces'. You can reliably put a figure on time, materials and the other relevant costs but how do you cost inspiration, your technical skill, creative design skill, experience and knowledge? It's not easy!

It's a touchy area to attempt to define production versus one-off craft art pieces. We distinguish between work which has a high degree of personal input and originality of design (and so cannot normally be made using production methods) and work which (theoretically at least) could be made using production techniques. Consider the items you could make (even if you don't) by rapid production methods. A potter throwing mugs, or casting moulds is a clear cut example, yours may not be!

Try to establish a consistent pricing policy. One craftsperson we know claims to adjust his hourly rate to that of the profession of his client, but there are less unconventional methods. Here are a couple to give the idea.

There are 52 weeks in a year. Allowing for weekends, holidays and illness then, say, 45 weeks are left. Not all time is productive, so allow say 36 weeks of actual productive working time. If you work a 50 hour week then multiply 50 x 36 = 1,800 hours available per year. Decide how much you need to earn a year and match your hourly rate to this income. Using this example it takes $10 per hour to earn $18,000 a year and so on.

Another approach is to start with the set hourly rate in mind. For a particular piece, work out the time taken, add a bit for lost time spent and multiply by the hourly rate you want. Incorporating material costs and overheads will give you a basis for setting wholesale prices to your work.

For example, a potter takes 1 hour to make an urn, and she adds another hour for her work other than throwing, giving a total time of 2 hours per urn.

She thinks $10 an hour is a fair wage 2 x $10 = $20

Overheads and materials cost her $500 per week or $10 per hour and she works a 50 hour week, so cost per item $10 x 2 = $20

| | | |
|---|---|---|
| Labour: 2 hours @ $10 | = | 20 |
| Overheads & materials: 2 hours @ $10 | = | 20 |
| Wholesale price of urn: | = | $40 |

Whatever method you adopt will have to be fine-tuned for your own situation. Overhead costs are often forgotten! In establishing a pricing policy or at least some ground rules for yourself, add in all overheads as well as your direct material costs and time. The wholesale price is a more consistent marker than retail, and should represent fair compensation for your efforts, both technical and creative. Wholesale prices are most often the minimum return you can receive for your work which covers your costs and provides a margin (your profit). If you are primarily a recreational craft artist you may feel comfortable asking for very low, even 'below cost' prices for your pieces, but this is unwise and unethical. A fair and realistic price is made to appear extortionate in the customers' eyes as you've adjusted their expectations downwards. It can help to look at prices of comparable work in galleries or shops.

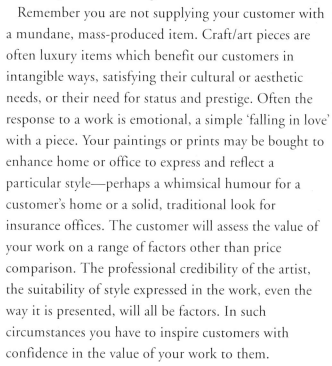

# THE PRICE
# OF GENIUS?

So much for production, what about the thorny problem of setting the prices of 'designer' works. One suggestion is to allow a higher hourly rate to account for time taken in experimenting with new designs. Alternatively you might opt to count all time spent, including designing and sketching prototypes at the basic hourly rate.

Our stance is that those one off pieces which 'work' have to cover for the pieces that don't make it. Inevitably there will be fuzzy areas—the piece which sings warrants a respectable price, even if conception and execution were rapid. If you think you've put a little bit of inspirational genius in a piece, then charge for that special something!

Remember you are not supplying your customer with a mundane, mass-produced item. Craft/art pieces are often luxury items which benefit our customers in intangible ways, satisfying their cultural or aesthetic needs, or their need for status and prestige. Often the response to a work is emotional, a simple 'falling in love' with a piece. Your paintings or prints may be bought to enhance home or office to express and reflect a particular style—perhaps a whimsical humour for a customer's home or a solid, traditional look for insurance offices. The customer will assess the value of your work on a range of factors other than price comparison. The professional credibility of the artist, the suitability of style expressed in the work, even the way it is presented, will all be factors. In such circumstances you have to inspire customers with confidence in the value of your work to them.

You are a customer too. What do you look for when the buyer/seller roles are reversed? Generally a customer

Barry and Dianne Wood's pottery studio
Craig Potton

is looking for value, and this is not the same as price. Listening to customer feedback will confirm this. To illustrate, someone who buys an artistic piece may choose it for its beauty—how can anyone define this quantitatively!

Fairness and consistency of pricing is very important and by now you will realise that pricing is not the clear-cut subject you might expect. As with everything, you'll get better with experience. Pricing is, of necessity, an individual formula. You are selling your skills, a part of yourself if you like.

## PROFITS
## (OR... WHAT THE OUTSIDE
## WORLD PROVIDES IN RETURN)

Profits keep you and your creative enterprise in good heart. Profits enable you to enhance your working life, and allow you to choose the work you want to do. Craft artists are fairly reluctant to go wholeheartedly after profit, feeling that it is an unacceptably commercial perspective which runs counter to their creative skills. We'd argue that if you are selling a high quality beautiful object it should be valued accordingly!

Almost inevitably (unless you are independently wealthy or incredibly lucky) you will start as the classic struggling artist! The financial rewards will be small and the commitment of time and energy colossal. This state of affairs is normal in the short term—but it should not go on indefinitely. A fair recompense for your work should be within your reach without having to work from dawn to dusk 365 days a year!

We'll consider here approaches that different craft artists adopt to ensure reasonable profit for a reasonable effort (what 'reasonable' means is up to the individual). One very basic way to enhance profits is to minimise costs. See if items you buy from retail outlets are available from the manufacturers. Almost invariably, the more materials you buy, the relatively cheaper per unit it becomes. If you cannot use vast quantities you could buy in conjunction with others if the savings warrant it. Cooperative buying is also a way to use suppliers who are reluctant to deal in small (uneconomic to them) quantities.

Working more efficiently is another way to enhance profits. Your time is, after all, of increasing value as you learn and therefore become more skilled! Working

Care and attention to detail—remember that you are not supplying
your customers with a mundane mass-produced piece.

efficiently does not mean quick, slap-dash working, rather it means considered,
non-wasteful effort, effectively applied. Planning your work will minimise non-
productive time and (non-creative time) and your profits will rise!

Can you lower accountancy costs by taking on more of the responsibility
yourself? Sympathetic accountants will help you establish systems that you can
handle. Doing monthly accounts also lets you know how things are going
without having recourse to experts to find out if news is good or bad! Apart
from the self-confidence boost you get from learning to cope with such matters,
you have the added bonus that it hasn't cost you a fee!

In simplistic terms, profit is the difference between what you earn and what
you spend. That being so, it's timely to consider that large egos cost a lot to
feed. The trap of wanting to fit a particular image has caught a few craft artists.
The 'does it earn its keep' test has to be applied. Most of us have to make
compromises. In the early days particularly, when tight finances are usually part
of the scene, a little conservatism is called for, even if it's out of character! There
may come times when your instinct tells you to go for it, but you can't let this
happen too often if you and your creative enterprise are to flourish!

# ENJOYING THE LIFESTYLE

*IN THIS CHAPTER WE TAKE A CLOSER look at our chosen lifestyle as craft artists. It may be true that nothing worthwhile is ever easy, but with some thought craft artists can have the ultimate lifestyle — that of working at what is enjoyable, and being paid to do so.*

As a professional craft artist you should be committed to creating well made and beautiful objects, whether one-offs, or production work. To become a happy, well-rounded, successful craft artist you need to maintain a balance between the different aspects of your life. In what follows we shall look at ways craft artists have achieved a happy balance both in their life and in their life's work.

A major key to lifestyle satisfaction is becoming comfortable with and appreciating the value of areas of work which involve technical expertise and elements of repetition. With this in mind we look at ways craft artists can deal with this and still maintain their artistic drive.

Ultimately the way you decide to work and live is over to you. What constitutes the ideal lifestyle is going to vary with different personalities and aspirations. The thing is to aim for the lifestyle you want, on terms that you personally find acceptable and agreeable.

## MAINTAINING ENTHUSIASM

To earn a living craft artists must extend their horizons and accept the challenge of making both a life's work and a livelihood from their creative ability. We can accept the need for integrity in our work but it can take a long time to accept that the value of our work is not diminished by becoming equally skilled in producing and marketing that work.

Many of us daydream about an ideal existence where we are freed from external pressure and can just 'make our art', but mental doodling isn't enough—you have to be productive too. Being a success and a good craft artist isn't a matter of lucky breaks, sometimes it's not even a matter of skills. Much hinges on attitude, not what happens to you along the way, but more what you do with it! Considered in the right way, even your learned business acumen can be a creative quality. You don't have to be poor to maintain integrity and artistic credibility, whatever you hear to the contrary.

Keeping your interest from flagging is at the heart of maintaining balance. You could become outstandingly successful yet loathe it if the interest has gone for you. Conversely your creative genius might flounder in a sort of artistic vacuum if you cannot come to grips with guiding your inspiration!

Enjoying what you do is easy when things are going well, and with a little effort craft artists can generally ensure that they do.

### Handling routine

Many craft artists still worry that applying efficent production techniques to their work will somehow impede their creative flow. It won't. Craft artists generally find their skills enhanced by the practice of routine repetitive work— they become closer to their medium, they develop a sure rhythm and confidence with their chosen materials, they feel better able to overcome design problems that previously came between them and their medium through the fluency gained by familiarity. Remember that routine and repetition are common in many other fields, after all dancers constantly practise at the barre, and musicians their scales.

The skills gained in production work will always aid your professional development as a craft artist. Once you know what you can achieve with your enhanced technical skills you become more relaxed in style and, because you know so well what you can do in the medium, you are not diverted by technical matters when designing. Some new craft artists try too hard to be over elaborate, or technically clever, and the outcome can be aesthetically unfortunate—in other words their designs don't work. After an 'apprenticeship' of experience, older and wiser craft artists develop their own individual design sense and create more effective work. They have not lost their creative flair or vision, merely learned their trade.

However, there's no getting around the fact that routine, repetitive tasks can at times be more than a little tedious. So how do you beat the tedium? Essentially the trick is in finding out what suits your style and your particular situation. Some craft artists set themselves time goals and try to beat the clock by making more items in each time period. It works for a lot of craft artists when faced with a large order; a local potter friend survives making endless domestic ware in this way! The clock game is not the approach for everyone though, and you may dislike the extra pressure, even where it is self-imposed and illusory.

Another way of handling routine is to break the task down to more acceptable

Photo: Craig Potton

segments which you can work through in small bites between more appealing tasks. Some craft artists find this tactic helps maintain their interest level.

Maintaining enthusiasm often hinges on striking a balance in the format of your work that suits you personally. If you are lucky enough (or astute enough) for example to find a niche market that you can satisfy happily and profitably then interest is unlikely to pall. But if the demand for your work increases to the point where you seem to work every hour of every day in order to keep up, any pleasure will be soon lost.

Sure you'll be caught out now and again and will have to put on an extra spurt of effort; a certain measure of greed comes into it when you can see all those bills paid or visualise that new equipment just waiting to be picked up. Stretching yourself in this way won't do any damage now and again, but don't overdo it. Learn to recognise when you are ready for a change of pace.

A little pressure of deadlines can be challenging—adrenaline isn't only for sportspeople and it's always a good feeling to have achieved what you set out to do even if it's simply a matter of preparing all of a shop order by a promised due date. We all need to know what conditions suit us best, and how and when we do our best work. Some craft artists like to completely separate their production work from time devoted to art pieces. Others happily flit from one approach to the other.

## MAINTAINING YOUR INSPIRATION

Craft artists who worry about losing creative flow or having their ideas dry up on them may just be looking at the problem from the wrong angle. Getting ideas isn't usually the real problem, it's managing to hold on to them that's difficult! Ideas come at the oddest and most inconvenient times. How many times has a great idea come to you in the shower or in the middle of the night! Ideas for brilliant designs you dreamt up and forgot by morning won't make your name for you!

If this sounds familiar, consider a new approach. Be prepared to note down your elusive ideas straight away. Many craft artists swear by a scrapbook which they have to hand for snippets that they may someday use. A collection of notes, sketches and memos to which they can refer as resource material. The designated scrapbook offers a better chance of being able to locate the written or drawn reminder of that germ of an idea and being able to decipher it months later, but in any case, get it down, even if you just scribble on backs of envelopes or whatever is to hand.

Recycle good ideas too. A mistake we've committed in the past is failing to sketch or photograph one of our own designs that appealed. Learn from our mistakes—if there's a piece of work you've made which really grabs you, then make a sketch or take a photo before it leaves your studio (and possibly your memory) for ever!

Always be receptive to new ideas. Often when we're engaged in particular tasks we have to focus on what we're doing and ideas that pop up are an irrelevance we push aside. Jot the idea down or sketch it, then return to the task. Work efficiency is not just a matter of working hard. You'll find it pays to pace yourself. Pressure, whether imposed by yourself or by outside circumstances, should not be a constant factor in your work. Make sure you fully understand that efficiency is not the same as continually working without let up!

Some craft artists deliberately put aside time away from 'proper work' in their studio for relaxed dabbling with no particular aim in mind and find this generates ideas for new directions. We're talking here of trying short breaks, to see if they induce a more receptive frame of mind rather than encouraging you to become a bankrupt layabout! You may not seem to achieve much but this occasional change of pace and impetus could be worthwhile. Any relaxation period seems to be useful in offering an unstructured environment free of normal limitations.

Craft artists frequently develop ideas from unlikely sources of inspiration. Influences from books, films, magazines and television can set off a train of thought to pursue. Perhaps thumbing through magazines that you wouldn't normally read in your dentist's waiting room will throw up some gems. After all, for the next half hour or so in his surgery chair you can't talk, so you might as well use the time to plan, design and dream—the gas may even help!

Browsing through books on crafts, antiques, architecture and fine arts can be quite enjoyable, although it may also be disheartening at times to see your wonderful 'new' design displayed in a photograph of a Victorian interior! We viewed a new ceramics exhibition which the catalogue described as showing latest designs of top ceramicists. By chance we later passed a bookstore in whose window was displayed a special promotion of Art Deco books. Lo and behold, the new ceramics would have been quite at home in the 1930's photographs. Similarly primitive artifacts viewed in museums may inspire designs in modern materials.

Like the message of anecdote, transforming changes occur in these designs so the resemblance is a point of interest rather than censure. Using resources in this way is not a matter of copying someone else's ideas, rather of being open to influence from a wide range of sources.

Exhibitions can be a valuable spur for ideas and enthusiasm. Preparing for a group or sole exhibition can be a great incentive to the craft artist to strive to produce a new body of work, perhaps even a change in direction from current works. One gallery owner we know stages exhibitions through the year. Some

Woven flax by Susan Barrett

*Julia Brooke-White*

are media orientated, so that, for example, metalworkers are invited to exhibit separately from other craft artists. Often though, she will set a theme and all gallery suppliers are invited to submit works. This sort of market-led inspiration can be a lot of fun!

Exhibitions carry a risk factor in that your work is exposed for evaluation and criticism in a more public format than you might normally experience. This is all to the good. Flattering friends and relatives who think that all your work is wonderful are great as a support base, but won't ever push you to do better. At the same time there's no future in being overawed by some of the gallery work you view—all you can ask of yourself is that you do the best you can within your current abilities. (Remembering that these change with time!).

Preparing and selecting work to submit for exhibition, and the constructive criticism you receive through exhibiting work, will aid your growth as a craft artist. New enthusiasm in developing a personal style in your work can be generated by preparing pieces specially for exhibition.

The market generally, will help the craft artist to keep ideas and enthusiasm running high. A new type of commission work can be a stimulating exercise. For example, a client may want garden decorations and other outdoor forms outside your normal sphere of work. The new ideas could develop into an interesting project for you. Perhaps some exhibition ideas will result, or a totally new line of work. This is a time when your notebook and/or camera should be put to good use so that as good ideas arise they are not mislaid!

Design competitions can offer a further market-led design spur. An excellent competition was recently staged by an Australian tourism board which invited craftspeople to design a good quality, handmade souvenir—a response, it would seem, to the tacky imports flooding the 'Australiana' market. The design briefs were very specific, even stipulating the retail price band for each section of the contest. Of the winning entries, what was most impressive was the variety of solutions brought to the design problems the entrants faced. There is little doubt that such events are good for generating new ideas and approaches to your work.

Finally in this section, we should mention the importance of developing and retaining enthusiasm for the business side of your venture. Don't worry about lack of experience; business sense is mostly common sense, and what you don't know you'll learn. Craft artists often worry about their ability in this area so developing enthusiasm here would save a lot of angst. Even if you consider yourself the antithesis of a business personality, you will cope.

Marketing is not just for big businesses. If you don't market your work, or have someone do it for you, then you are going to rely heavily on chance opportunities. We all get the odd lucky break (we trust) but by and large most of us have to work at it. Permit yourself to take a lively interest in marketing and your creative enterprise will flourish. We all have different drives and motivations, just ensure that yours provides a balance of hard work, efficiency and fun!

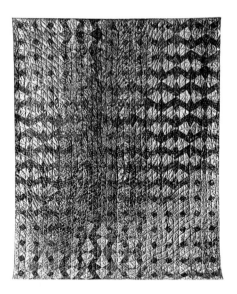

# COMMON PROBLEMS

*IN THIS CHAPTER WE LOOK at how craft artists have dealt with common problems that arise in a craft art venture. You may not be at the stage where you need their cautionary tales, or perhaps their woes won't apply to you. But just in case, craft artists share some hard-won lessons that will help you keep happily afloat.*

## MONEY

**M**oney, or more specifically, getting paid, is a common difficulty craft artists face. Craft art ventures tend to be small and are therefore extremely vulnerable if even one or two big customers default on payment for work.

Major art commissions may seem like your big chance, but in practice some turn out to be very bad news indeed. Artistic commissions unfortunately provide horrific examples of unsatisfactory payment arrangements. One mural artist we know spent fifteen months recovering all the costs due to him from a major commission. If the prestige of the commission is worth the risk of low, even no payment, you may still decide to take it on. You may feel that this commission will be such a boost for your career that you'll grab it with both hands whatever the return—that choice should be made with open eyes!

Large corporate commissions can bring their own set of problems in that you may be talking to an agency rather than with the client directly, and misunderstandings can arise. Ideally people will abide by what they've said. Realistically, they can equally well deny they said any such thing! Some clients or representatives, whilst themselves well paid, curiously seem to expect the craft artist to work for artistic gratification alone! If you want to ensure you are fairly compensated, even at the risk of losing the commission, then be professional. Unless you are confident of, and preferably have worked with the client previously, then ask for written confirmations. Remember that a verbal contract isn't worth anything. If you don't get what you want in writing then do it yourself. Set down clearly what you understood from the meeting with the client or client representative. Clarify what work you are going to do for them and when, and also what you expect to be paid and when. Send this to the client for response. With written evidence of the agreement you're in a position of strength.

Chasing up overdue payments is often unpleasant, but must be done. Steel yourself to make that phonecall or send that letter. Inefficient bookkeeping isn't confined to craftspeople and a reminder may be all it takes. Only experience will help you sort out a genuine temporary cashflow difficulty from a hardened slow payer. If you feel that it's worth your while to go the extra mile for your client, perhaps payment by instalments or a similar compromise will work for

'Shell Series' decorated by Gloria Young, pots by Rachel Vollush           *Julia Brooke-White*

you. The important thing is to address the problem rather than let it fester

Only rarely are payment problems the fault of the craft artist; there are only occasional instances where the craft artist fails to provide a clear invoice or sends illegible statements with their consigned work to shops or galleries. Surprisingly, ostensibly sound, major customers, deliberately avoid or delay payment as a regular policy. With this in mind aim to check new clients to ensure they don't fit into this category. You can usually ask other craft artists and be guided by what they say, or what they don't say. There is normally an efficient grapevine in operation! We have (unwisely in retrospect) supplied such customers in the past when we felt we needed them. On balance the income was not worth the hassle of constantly niggling for payment on every order. Irritatingly, such outlets are often a good source of income for craft artists, if you can force payment. The squeaky wheels get the oil, so ensure your payment becomes a priority with such clients.

Resolve never to supply an order until full payment for the previous order has been received and banked. Have a bottom line of this sort and mean it! You may be an absolutely fabulous craft artist but you won't do well if you don't get paid for your wonderful creations.

Payment problems can be resolved if there is goodwill on both sides—if there isn't, get the money you are owed and cross them off your list.

Still on the money theme make sure you keep track of how everything is going close to home. If you start to exceed your overdraft limit, if you can't pay your own bills on time, if an application that you've made for extra credit or loan facilities has been denied—then reappraise your situation. It is a good idea to keep a regular if informal tally of your income and costs. Compare them to previous months, accumulate the figures to give a running total (draw up a chart if you prefer a picture to look at).

A good general policy is to bank income straight away, but pay out bills once a month so that any bill after your 'paying day' has to wait till next month. This habit ensures you have money coming in before you write out your payment cheques, and you save time by writing all your cheques at one time. Taxation problems often stem from poor record-keeping, so there's plenty of motivation there for you to make a reasonable job of your books!

## IMAGE ANXIETY

Not all the problems craft artists encounter relate so directly to money. Image can be a knotty problem too! Many craft artists find themselves dismissed as 'lifestylers' or considered slightly dim by business people with whom they have dealings. Different craft artists have their own reactions to this brushoff treatment which is perhaps best ignored as something which goes with the territory. Just grit your teeth and console yourself that very many of those 'proper' businesses have huge debt burdens behind those high street windows, so why would you want to emulate them?

One craft artist conceded that his image anxiety led him to overextend on expensive brochures, equipment and display material. Image does matter, but feeding a big ego gets expensive. Know the difference and check that your spending is justifiable.

# DEALING POSITIVELY
# WITH BAD SITUATIONS

If the worst happens and you make some blunders, what can you do to get out of the mess? Often the first instinct is to ignore the problem and work longer and harder in the hope that you can somehow work your way out of the difficulty. It may work but does not usually treat the problem itself. Longer hours and superhuman efforts may help in the short term but it's better to stop and resolve the problem while you still have energy to cope! Especially if your personal life is suffering, then stop and think. If you carry on unchanged the situation is unlikely to resolve itself.

Rules one to ten: If you're in a bad situation, get out of it. Brooding or panic won't change things. Talking to an outside person might. They need not be an expert, just a fresh eye on your problem. Suggestions they offer may show a way out of the bad situation. The following cases illustrate some problems that craft artists face, and hopefully resolve. Bear in mind that with bad luck, as with good, it's not so much what happens to you as what you do about it, that counts.

Two examples:

The craftsperson in this example developed his jewellery venture from an enjoyable art form into a good living with the help of his spouse. His jewellery sold readily to local stores. They lived in a tourist destination and over the holiday season things went so well they took on staff to help with finishing work. As the season ended though, shop orders diminished. They still had staff to pay and their other debts began to mount up. It seemed they had gone from boom to bust.

The situation was serious enough for them to decide to stop and give themselves breathing space to completely re-evaluate their position. Together, with the help of an acquaintance who ran an unrelated business, they summarised what in retrospect seemed obvious—that sales peaked in a holiday season which meant a heavy work load for a short time, but after that, sales were slow and paying staff for whom there was no work meant inroads into funds so bills were left unpaid.

Next the jeweller and his spouse talked over their feelings and found they enjoyed working together and the jeweller himself still loved the creative work.

Both just wished it paid better and were willing to seek advice and act upon it.

Armed with new awareness they tackled the problems. Having established the seasonal nature of sales, they set out to plan his work so that they could build up stock in quiet periods. They decided to employ staff for the holiday season only because this was a better option than having insufficient work at times, and too much at others. Their strategy worked because the better use of staff enabled work to be completed efficiently and their debts more easily resolved.

The second example concerns a successful potter who sustained a bad shoulder injury while skiing. Her injury kept her off the wheel for months, and the long recuperation period meant that she was unable to return to the same punishing work of hours of throwing pots. In desperation to earn, she had moulds made for outdoor planters. Fortuitously her accident coincided with the current trend in garden fashion to the extent that she has now altered the style of her potting completely. Her partner, while no potter himself, assists with the donkey work associated with mould preparation and finishing. She has diversified her work so has a manageable amount of throwing which doesn't overtax her body. In solving a problem, she has developed a positive new direction in her work.

In both these cases, despite encountering difficulties, the craft artists went from strength to strength. They did this by dealing positively with a bad situation in which others might have given up.

It needn't take a major upset though to make us aware of the virtue of planning, thinking and assessing what we are doing and what we want to do in the foreseeable future. Rethinking and re-evaluating can be immensely helpful to the craft artist: Has your approach to your work changed? Do you have the same feeling of achievement? Have your goals altered? Taking stock of where you're at and where you'd like to be every so often is a valuable exercise. You may well make modifications in the light of new goals you set as a result, even those as simple as "getting out more as I never talk to anyone but other painters, potters, weavers"!

## FINDING BALANCE BETWEEN CREATIVITY AND BUSINESS

Craft artists should aim not only for excellence in their chosen craft, but also in business, relishing the challenge this provides. But coming to terms with business has been a major problem for many craft artists. By putting your mind to it, this issue—that of living and working by sucessfully marketing your work—can be resolved.

If our customers and other contacts are anything to go by, and talking with other craft artists seems to indicate they are, then the general consensus is that anyone could do what you're doing if they had the time. A friend who writes novels hears the same sentiment expressed regularly. Well yes, anyone can (theoretically) do anything (how well is another matter). But there's far more involved than 'just having the time'.

Those craft artists who don't appreciate this set out on an enterprise full of confidence until they strike the first (inevitable) hurdle. Thereupon they swing to the other extreme. From "anyone could…" it becomes "I can't manage", "I'm an artist I don't 'do' business" or the face-saving chestnut, "my work isn't commercial". Because it hasn't been the breeze they anticipated, then it all seems to disintegrate. Earning a living as a craft artist must just be for hardened commercial types! Not!

The truth is that as a practising craft artist you need a balance. Ups and downs are inevitable, normal, and to be expected, even if they are not anticipated.

Accept this, and you really can do anything. Having fun and maintaining that first flush of enthusiasm with which you started is important. Achieving this will support you against the downs which are part and parcel of any enterprise.

Earning a living as a craft artist is more than just deriving a source of income—it's a part of your day-to-day experience, and it makes sense therefore, to ensure that the experience is as congenial as it can possibly be. When things go wrong don't take it as a personal affront. The odd hiccup in your venture is bound to happen, and dealing with these glitches will teach you a lot.

What line and level of creative venture you want to pursue is over to you; know what you want to achieve and what you are happy with. Success isn't a matter of being top dog, it's being able to enjoy your own unique achievements, being fulfilled in your chosen work and being generally contented and pleased with your lot! In whatever direction you take, developing confidence and competence in business positively contributes to your personal abilities. Our examples demonstrate clearly how others have been able to resolve their differing needs and aspirations.

No craft artist should feel unable to tackle the professional side. Being businesslike is largely a matter of commonsense and good manners. Frankly, if you are a pain to deal with and won't meet people halfway it's likely your experiences will be negative. Try to balance your essential belief in your ability with recognition that sometimes you'll have to ask others to help you, and sometimes you may have to adjust your ideas and expectations.

Everything that we have covered here is within the capability of the motivated craft artist. Operating a craft art venture can and should be stimulating, fulfilling and rewarding. It is sad that so many craft artists leave art school or other courses feeling that the only way to make a living is by teaching. Fine if you want to teach, but what a lousy choice from everyone's standpoint if you think it is all you are fit for!

Good work, professional ethics and attitudes will ensure you survive and flourish as a craft artist. Accept and enjoy. We wish you happiness and continued success.

One-fifth scale model of hall console table by Vic Matthews.
*Julia Brooke-White*

# INDEX